# A Touch of
# HOME

A Collection of Recipes from the Friends of The Samaritan Inn

# *A Touch of* HOME

## A Collection of Recipes from the Friends of The Samaritan Inn

Published by The Samaritan Inn

ISBN:  978-0-9789805-0-4

Edited, Designed, and Manufactured by

**Community**Classics™

An imprint of

P. O. Box 305142
Nashville, Tennessee 37230
(800) 358–0560

Manufactured in China
First Printing: 2007
5,000 copies

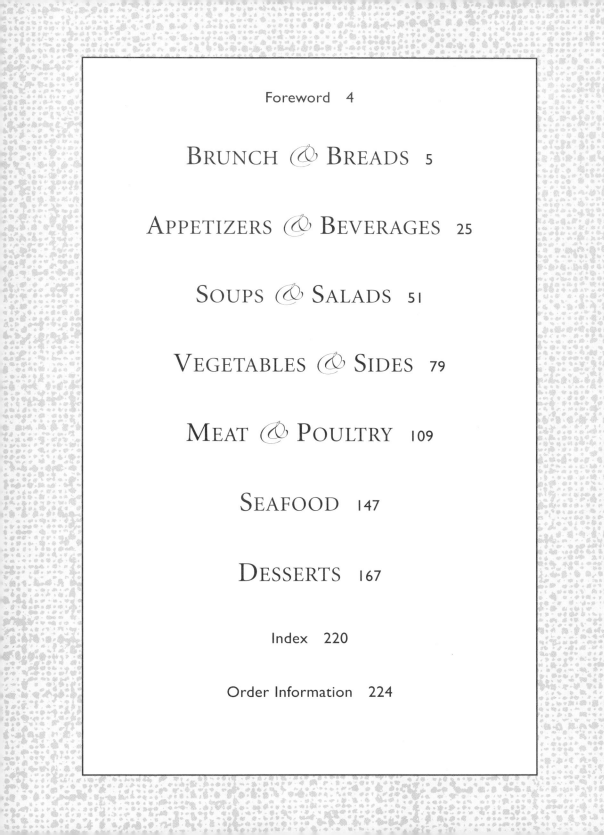

# ABOUT THE SAMARITAN INN

The Samaritan Inn, a facility serving the homeless,
was established in 1984 with a goal of helping families
and individuals regain their independence.

It starts with a place to stay—clean, safe, three meals
a day, with shower and laundry facilities, a computer lab,
and a playground for children.

It continues with professional Case Managers who
meet with each resident to help him or her develop a
plan that will lead to independence and who then
regularly reviews his or her progress.

It culminates when residents "graduate" from the
Inn and set up their own households. Ongoing support
is provided even then to help ensure that their
independence is permanent.

The Samaritan Inn is a nonprofit corporation
that depends on financial contributions from individuals,
churches, corporations, grants, foundations,
and United Way.

# BRUNCH
# & BREADS

# SLOW-COOKER BRUNCH CASSEROLE

1 pound bulk pork sausage
1 dozen eggs
1 cup milk
Salt and pepper to taste
1 (32-ounce) package frozen hash brown potatoes
1 onion, chopped
1 pound bacon, crisp-cooked and crumbled
4 cups (16 ounces) shredded cheese

Brown the sausage in a skillet, stirring until crumbly; drain. Beat the eggs, milk, salt and pepper in a mixing bowl until smooth. Layer the potatoes, onion, sausage, bacon and cheese one-half at a time in a large slow cooker. Pour the egg mixture over the top. Cook on Low for 10 to 12 hours or until the eggs are cooked through.

*Becky James*

# SUNDAY BRUNCH CASSEROLE

8 ounces sliced bacon
1/2 cup chopped onion
1/2 cup chopped green bell pepper
1 dozen eggs
1 cup milk
1 (16-ounce) package frozen hash brown potatoes, thawed
1 cup (4 ounces) shredded Cheddar cheese
1 teaspoon salt
1/2 teaspoon pepper
1/4 teaspoon dill weed

Cook the bacon in a large skillet over medium heat until crisp.
Remove the bacon to paper towels to drain; crumble. Drain the
skillet, reserving 2 tablespoons of the drippings. Sauté the onion
and bell pepper in the reserved drippings in the skillet until tender;
drain. Whisk the eggs and milk in a large bowl until well blended.
Stir in the potatoes, cheese, salt, pepper, dill weed, onion mixture
and crumbled bacon. Pour into a greased 9×13-inch baking dish.
Bake, uncovered, at 350 degrees for 35 to 45 minutes or until a
knife inserted near the center comes out clean.

*Megan Sullivan*

# TATER TOT CASSEROLE

1 pound ground beef
1 small onion, chopped
1 (10-ounce) can cream of mushroom soup
2 tablespoons sour cream (optional)
1 (28-ounce) package frozen Tater Tots
Shredded Cheddar cheese

Brown the ground beef with the onion in a skillet, stirring until the ground beef is crumbly; drain. Combine the ground beef mixture with the soup and sour cream in a bowl and mix well. Pour into a baking dish. Spread the Tater Tots over the top and sprinkle with cheese. Cover with foil and bake at 350 degrees for 30 minutes. Remove the foil and broil until the Tater Tots are crisp and golden brown.

*Becky James*


# CORN AND SAUSAGE SKILLET

1 pound bulk pork sausage
2 tablespoons all-purpose flour
1 1/2 cups milk
1 (15-ounce) can whole kernel corn, drained

Brown the sausage in a skillet, stirring until crumbly. Drain the sausage, reserving 1 tablespoon of the drippings. Stir the flour into the reserved drippings in the skillet. Cook over medium heat until brown, stirring constantly. Stir in the milk gradually. Cook until thickened, stirring constantly. Return the sausage to the skillet and stir in the corn. Simmer for 5 minutes.

*Kerri Coffin*

# Ham and Egg Casserole

1 dozen eggs
1 cup sour cream
1 cup chopped cooked ham
6 ounces Monterey Jack cheese, shredded
Minced onion to taste
1 (4-ounce) can chopped green chiles
1 tablespoon parsley flakes
Shredded Cheddar cheese

Process the eggs and sour cream in a blender until smooth. Layer the ham and Monterey Jack cheese in a greased 9×13-inch baking dish. Pour the egg mixture over the Monterey Jack cheese. Mix the onion, green chiles and parsley in a small bowl and sprinkle over the egg mixture. Top with Cheddar cheese. Bake at 350 degrees for 45 minutes.

*Kerri Coffin*

# EGGS FOR BRUNCH

4 1/2 slices bread
Chopped Canadian bacon or ham (optional)
12 ounces Cheddar cheese, shredded
6 eggs
3 cups milk
3/4 teaspoon salt
3/4 teaspoon dry mustard

Cut the bread slices into 1-inch squares and arrange in a single layer in a greased 9×13-inch baking dish. Sprinkle with Canadian bacon and the Cheddar cheese. Combine the eggs, milk, salt and mustard in a mixing bowl and beat until smooth. Pour over the cheese. Cover and chill for 10 to 12 hours. Bake, uncovered, at 325 degrees for 1 hour. Serve with sautéed mushrooms.

*Florence Brady Stanton and Mary Kay Brady*


# BAKED EGG IN A TOAST CUP

1 slice bread
1 egg
Salt and pepper to taste
1/2 teaspoon butter

Trim the crust from the bread. Press the bread gently into a greased custard cup or muffin cup so that the corners extend to the top of the cup. Break the egg into the cup. Sprinkle with salt and pepper and top with the butter. Bake at 400 degrees for 15 minutes.

*Marla Storm*

# CHEESY HAM CUPS

1 (10-count) can refrigerator flaky biscuits
3-ounces cream cheese, softened
1 cup chopped cooked ham
Sliced black olives (optional)
4 ounces Cheddar cheese, shredded
1 (4-ounce) can chopped green chiles, drained

Separate the biscuit dough and press firmly into muffin cups coated with nonstick cooking spray, forming cups. Combine the cream cheese, ham, olives, Cheddar cheese and green chiles in a large bowl and mix well. Spoon the cream cheese mixture into the cups. Bake at 350 degrees for 15 to 20 minutes or until golden brown.

*Brian Shelton*

# PORTOBELLO CHEESE SANDWICH

4 portobello mushroom caps
4 red bell peppers, seeded and cut into quarters
Italian salad dressing
4 sandwich rolls or buns, cut into halves
4 slices provolone cheese
Baby spinach leaves, rinsed and trimmed

Rinse the mushroom caps and pat dry. Place the mushroom caps and bell peppers on a baking sheet and brush with a small amount of salad dressing. Broil until tender and slightly charred. Slice the mushroom caps and bell peppers and place equal portions on the bottom half of each roll. Top with the cheese. Microwave on High until the cheese is melted. Place spinach over the cheese and cover with the top halves of the rolls.

*Pamela Hathaway*

# Orange Pecan French Toast

1 cup packed brown sugar
1/3 cup butter, melted
2 tablespoons light corn syrup
1/3 cup chopped pecans
12 (3/4-inch) slices
   French bread
1 cup fresh orange juice
1 teaspoon grated orange zest

1/2 cup 2% milk
2 eggs
3 egg whites
3 tablespoons granulated sugar
1 teaspoon cinnamon
1 teaspoon vanilla extract
1 tablespoon
   confectioners' sugar

Stir the brown sugar, butter and corn syrup together in a small bowl. Pour into a greased 9×13-inch baking dish and spread evenly over the bottom. Sprinkle the pecans over the brown sugar mixture. Arrange the bread slices close together in a single layer over the pecans. Whisk the orange juice, orange zest, milk, eggs, egg whites, granulated sugar, cinnamon and vanilla in a bowl. Pour the egg mixture over the bread, pressing down on the bread to absorb the liquid. Cover and chill for 1 to 12 hours. Uncover and let stand at room temperature for 20 minutes. Bake at 350 degrees for 35 minutes or until golden brown. Dust with the confectioners' sugar and serve.

*Megan Sullivan*

# BAKED APPLE SOUFFLÉS

1/4 cup (1/2 stick) butter
1/3 cup packed brown sugar
1 apple, peeled and sliced
1 cup pancake mix
2/3 cup milk
2 tablespoons vegetable oil
1 egg, beaten

Melt the butter in a small skillet. Add the brown sugar and apple.
Heat until the brown sugar dissolves, stirring constantly. Pour
the apple mixture into two soufflé dishes coated with nonstick
cooking spray. Place the soufflé dishes on a baking sheet and
heat in a 350-degree oven until the dishes are hot. Combine the
pancake mix, milk, oil and egg in a bowl and mix well. Pour evenly
over the apple mixture. Bake, uncovered, at 350 degrees for
12 to 17 minutes or until golden brown. Invert onto a serving
dish. Serve with maple syrup.

*Margaret Dorland*

# BLUEBERRY COFFEE CAKE

2 (15-ounce) packages blueberry muffin mix
2/3 cup all-purpose flour
2/3 cup sugar
1 teaspoon cinnamon
1/2 cup (1 stick) butter
1 cup slivered almonds

Prepare the muffin mix using the package directions. Pour the batter into a greased 9×13-inch baking pan. Combine the flour, sugar and cinnamon in a bowl. Cut in the butter until crumbly. Sprinkle over the batter and top with the almonds. Bake at 375 degrees until the coffee cake tests done.

*Florence Brady Stanton and Mary Kay Brady*

# CHEESE DANISH

2 (8-count) cans refrigerator crescent rolls
16 ounces cream cheese, softened
1 cup sugar
1 egg yolk
1 teaspoon lemon juice
1 teaspoon almond extract
1 egg white, lightly beaten
1 cup sliced almonds
Confectioners' sugar

Unroll one can of the crescent roll dough and place in a 9×12-inch baking dish coated with nonstick cooking spray, pressing to cover the bottom. Combine the cream cheese, sugar, egg yolk, lemon juice and almond extract in a mixing bowl and beat until smooth. Spread over the dough. Unroll the remaining crescent roll dough on a sheet of waxed paper and roll into a 9×12-inch rectangle. Place over the cream cheese mixture. Brush the egg white over the top and then sprinkle with the almonds. Bake at 375 degrees for 25 minutes. Remove from the oven and sprinkle with confectioners' sugar.

For a Pecan Cheese Danish, use vanilla extract instead of almond extract and pecans instead of almonds. For a sweeter version, spread the first layer of dough with your favorite jelly or preserves before adding the cream cheese mixture.

*Margaret Dorland*

# Gooey Cinnamon Buns

4 cups bread flour
1 cup milk
1 egg, beaten
$1/4$ cup ($1/2$ stick)
  butter, melted
$1/4$ cup water
$1/2$ (4-ounce) package vanilla
  instant pudding mix
1 tablespoon granulated sugar
$2 1/4$ teaspoons bread
  machine yeast
$1/2$ teaspoon salt

1 cup packed brown sugar
$1/2$ cup (1 stick) butter, softened
2 teaspoons cinnamon
$1/4$ cup chopped walnuts
  (optional)
$1/4$ cup raisins (optional)
$1 1/2$ cups confectioners' sugar
$1/4$ cup ($1/2$ stick)
  butter, softened
1 teaspoon milk
1 teaspoon vanilla extract

Add the flour, 1 cup milk, the egg, $1/4$ cup melted butter, the water, pudding mix, granulated sugar, yeast and salt to the bread machine in the order recommended by the manufacturer. Set the machine on the dough mode. Remove the dough when the cycle is finished and knead for 3 to 5 minutes. Flatten into a large rectangle.

Mix the brown sugar, $1/2$ cup butter and the cinnamon in a small bowl. Spread over the dough. Sprinkle with the walnuts and raisins.
Roll the dough into a log, starting with the wide end of the rectangle; pinch to seal the seams. Cut into $1/2$- to 1-inch slices. Place on a greased 9×13-inch baking sheet and let rise until doubled in bulk. Bake at 350 degrees for 15 to 20 minutes or until golden brown.

Mix the confectioners' sugar, $1/4$ cup butter, 1 teaspoon milk and the vanilla in a small bowl until smooth. Spread over the warm rolls.

*Megan Sullivan*

# BANANA NUT BREAD

3 ripe bananas
1 teaspoon baking soda
2 cups all-purpose flour
1 1/2 cups sugar
1 cup (2 sticks) margarine, softened
3 eggs
1 teaspoon vanilla extract
1 cup finely chopped nuts

Mash the bananas in a small bowl. Stir in the baking soda and let stand. Combine the flour, sugar, margarine, eggs and vanilla in a mixing bowl and beat until smooth. Add the banana mixture and mix well. Stir in the nuts. Spoon into a greased and floured loaf pan. Bake at 350 degrees for 20 minutes. Reduce the oven temperature to 325 degrees and bake for 40 minutes longer.

*Kathy Filbert*

# STRAWBERRY BREAD

3 cups all-purpose flour
2 cups sugar
1 tablespoon cinnamon
1 teaspoon baking soda
$1/2$ teaspoon salt
1 cup vegetable oil
3 eggs, beaten
2 (10-ounce) packages frozen sliced strawberries, thawed

Combine the flour, sugar, cinnamon, baking soda and salt in a bowl and mix well. Mix the oil and eggs in a small bowl. Stir in the strawberries. Add the strawberry mixture to the dry ingredients and mix well. Pour the batter into two greased and floured 5×9-inch loaf pans. Bake at 350 degrees for 1 hour or until wooden picks inserted in the centers come out clean.

*Kerri Coffin*

# Strawberry Pecan Loaf

1 3/4 cups all-purpose flour
1 cup sugar
1 teaspoon baking soda
1/4 teaspoon salt
1/2 cup broken pecan halves
1/2 cup vegetable oil
2 eggs
1 (10-ounce) package frozen strawberries

Mix the flour, sugar, baking soda and salt in a bowl. Stir in the pecans. Combine the oil and eggs in a mixing bowl and beat until blended. Add the strawberries and beat at low speed just until the strawberries begin to break into pieces. Add the flour mixture and beat at low speed until the strawberries are in small pieces. Pour into a greased and lightly floured 5×9-inch loaf pan. Bake at 350 degrees for 1 hour or until the top is golden brown and the loaf pulls away from the sides of the pan. Cool in the pan for 10 minutes. Loosen the edges from the pan and invert onto a wire rack. Turn the loaf right side up and cool completely.

*Dawn Chaffee*

# ZUCCHINI BREAD

3 cups all-purpose flour
2$^1$/2 cups sugar
1$^1$/4 cups vegetable oil
4 eggs, beaten
4 teaspoons vanilla extract
1 tablespoon cinnamon
1$^1$/2 teaspoons salt
1$^1$/2 teaspoons baking soda
$^1$/2 teaspoon baking powder
4 cups coarsely shredded zucchini
1 cup chopped nuts (optional)

Combine the flour, sugar, oil, eggs, vanilla, cinnamon, salt, baking
soda and baking powder in a mixing bowl. Beat at low speed for
1 minute or until blended, scraping the side of the bowl constantly.
Add the zucchini and nuts and beat at medium speed for 1 minute.
Pour into two greased 5×9-inch loaf pans. Bake at 325 degrees for
50 to 60 minutes or until wooden picks inserted in the centers
come out clean. Cool in the pan for 10 minutes. Invert onto wire
racks to cool completely.

*Kathy Orwig*

# GARLIC CHEESE BISCUITS

2 cups baking mix
2/3 cup milk
1/2 cup (2 ounces) shredded Cheddar cheese
1/4 cup (1/2 stick) margarine, melted
1/4 teaspoon garlic powder

Combine the baking mix, milk and cheese in a mixing bowl and beat until a soft dough forms. Drop the dough by spoonfuls onto a baking sheet. Bake at 400 degrees for 8 to 10 minutes or until golden brown. Mix the margarine and garlic powder in a small bowl. Brush over the warm biscuits before removing from the baking sheet.

*Tracy Orwig*

# ROSEMARY AND ROASTED GARLIC BISCOTTI

1 1/3 cups all-purpose flour
1 teaspoon finely chopped
   fresh rosemary
1/2 teaspoon baking powder
1/2 teaspoon salt
1/2 cup sugar
1/2 cup (2 ounces) grated
   Romano cheese

1/2 cup extra-virgin olive oil
1 egg
1 egg yolk
1 teaspoon mashed roasted
   garlic (1 large clove)

Line a baking sheet with waxed paper or baking parchment. Combine the flour, rosemary, baking powder and salt in a bowl and mix well. Combine the sugar, cheese, olive oil, egg, egg yolk and garlic in a large mixing bowl and beat with the wire whisk attachment for 1 minute or until combined. Add the flour mixture and stir gently just until mixed. With damp hands, shape the dough into a log the length of the baking sheet and 3 inches wide. Place the log on the prepared baking sheet. Bake at 325 degrees for 30 minutes or until the log is firm and light brown. Remove from the oven and cool on the baking sheet for 5 minutes. Reduce the oven temperature to 250 degrees.

Place the log on a cutting board. Cut into 1/2-inch-thick slices using a sharp knife. Place the slices on a wire rack on top of the baking sheet and return to the oven. Bake for 30 minutes or until crisp and dry. Remove to a wire rack and cool completely before serving.

Biscotti may be stored in an airtight container for up to 2 weeks, or frozen in an airtight container for up to 6 weeks. The biscotti are excellent served with soups and salads, and are very tasty with chèvre (goat cheese) on top. For a more savory flavor, reduce the sugar to 1/4 cup.

*Deana Trones*

# CORN BREAD

1/4 cup shortening or
  vegetable oil
1 cup yellow cornmeal
1 cup all-purpose flour
4 teaspoons baking powder

1 tablespoon sugar
1/2 teaspoon salt
1 cup milk
1 egg, beaten

Melt the shortening in an ovenproof skillet in a 425-degree oven. Combine the cornmeal, flour, baking powder, sugar and salt in a bowl and mix well. Blend in the milk and egg. Add the hot shortening to the batter and mix well. Pour into the hot skillet and bake for 20 to 25 minutes or until golden brown.

*Nan Yancey*

# MEXICAN CORN BREAD

1 egg
1 cup buttermilk
3/4 cup cornmeal
1/4 cup all-purpose flour
2 teaspoons baking powder
1 teaspoon salt
1 teaspoon sugar
1/2 teaspoon baking soda

1 (8-ounce) can
  cream-style corn
2 teaspoons chopped
  jalapeño chile
1/2 cup (2 ounces)
  shredded cheese
2 tablespoons vegetable oil

Beat the egg in a mixing bowl. Add the buttermilk, cornmeal, flour, baking powder, salt, sugar and baking soda and beat until blended. Stir in the corn, jalapeño chile and cheese. Heat the oil in a baking pan in a 450-degree oven. Mix the hot oil into the batter. Pour the batter into the hot baking pan. Bake at 450 degrees for 20 minutes or until golden brown.

*Martha Cowan*

# APPETIZERS

## &

# BEVERAGES

# SHRIMP COCKTAIL WITH BLOODY MARY SORBET

1/4 cup water
3 tablespoons sugar
4 plum tomatoes, peeled,
  seeded and coarsely chopped
1/2 cup tomato juice
1 1/2 tablespoons tomato paste
1 tablespoon fresh lemon juice
Salt and pepper to taste
2 tablespoons minced
  fresh chives

Tabasco sauce to taste
18 fresh shrimp with tails,
  peeled and deveined
6 tablespoons sweetened
  lime juice
2 tablespoons dry vermouth
2 tablespoons sour cream
6 sprigs of cilantro
6 ribs celery with leafy tops

Combine the water and sugar in a small saucepan. Cook over medium heat until the sugar is dissolved, stirring constantly. Remove from the heat to cool. Process the sugar mixture, tomatoes, tomato juice, tomato paste, lemon juice, salt and pepper in a blender until smooth. Stir in the chives and Tabasco sauce. Pour into an ice cream freezer container and freeze using the manufacturer's instructions or freeze in a nonreactive baking dish until firm. Scrape the frozen sorbet into crystals using a fork.

Cook the shrimp in boiling water in a medium saucepan for about 2 minutes or until pink; drain. Rinse with cool water and pat dry.

Spoon the sorbet into six martini glasses. Spoon 1 tablespoon lime juice and 1 teaspoon vermouth into each glass. Top each serving with 1 teaspoon of the sour cream, a sprig of cilantro and a celery rib. Arrange three shrimp around the rim of each glass and serve.

*Deana Trones*

# BACON-WRAPPED PINEAPPLE SHRIMP

1/4 fresh pineapple, cut into bite-size pieces, or
   1 (14-ounce) can juice-pack pineapple chunks, drained
12 jumbo shrimp, peeled and deveined
6 slices center-cut bacon, cut into halves crosswise

Place a pineapple chunk in the curve of each shrimp. Wrap one piece of bacon around each shrimp and secure with a wooden pick. Cook in a hot nonstick skillet or on a griddle for 3 minutes on each side or until the bacon is crisp and the shrimp turn pink.

*Joni Shaw Smith*

# Asian Lettuce Wraps

1 pound ground pork, turkey or chicken
Minced garlic
1 tablespoon sesame oil
2 tablespoons hoisin sauce
1 tablespoon Sriracha sauce (Asian chile sauce)
1 tablespoon soy sauce
1 cup cilantro, chopped
2 or 3 green onions, chopped
1 (11-ounce) can mandarin oranges
1 (8-ounce) can water chestnuts
Lettuce leaves (Bibb, iceberg or romaine)

Brown the ground pork with garlic in the sesame oil in a skillet, stirring until the pork is crumbly. Stir in the hoisin sauce, Sriracha sauce and soy sauce. Add the cilantro, green onions, oranges and water chestnuts and stir to mix well. Cook until heated through. Place a portion of the hot pork mixture on a lettuce leaf and wrap the leaf around the filling to enclose. Garnish with additonal cilantro and green onions. Serve with additional Sriracha sauce to taste.

*Joni Shaw Smith*

# HOT DOG PIZZA-DILLAS

4 beef or pork hot dogs, cut into halves lengthwise
1 tablespoon extra-virgin olive oil
4 flour tortillas
Extra-virgin olive oil
1/4 cup mild chunky salsa
Ketchup
1 cup (4 ounces) shredded mozzarella or provolone cheese
1 cup (4 ounces) shredded Cheddar cheese

Slice each hot dog half into 1/2-inch pieces. Sauté the pieces in 1 tablespoon olive oil in a large nonstick skillet over medium-high heat for 2 to 4 minutes or until brown on all sides. Drain the hot dogs on a plate lined with paper towels and pour off any excess oil from the skillet.

For each pizza-dilla, cook a tortilla in a small amount of olive oil in the skillet over medium-high heat for 1 minute. Flip the tortilla over and reduce the heat to low. Spread 1 tablespoon of the salsa over half the tortilla. Add 2 squirts of ketchup and mix with the salsa. Sprinkle 1/4 cup of the mozzarella cheese and 1/4 cup of the Cheddar cheese over the salsa. Add one-fourth of the hot dog pieces. Fold the tortilla in half to cover the filling. Press down on the tortilla with a spatula. Cook for 1 minute per side. Remove to a serving plate and let stand for 2 minutes. Cut into four wedges.

*Chris Sale*

# Green Chile Pie

1 1/2 pounds ground round
1 onion, chopped
1 (10-ounce) can mild enchilada sauce
1 (10-ounce) can cream of chicken soup
1 (10-ounce) can cream of mushroom soup
1 1/2 cups sour cream
1 (7-ounce) can chopped green chiles
1 cup water
25 corn tortillas, cut into bite-size pieces
Shredded cheese

Brown the beef with the onion in a skillet, stirring until the beef is crumbly; drain. Combine the enchilada sauce, chicken soup, mushroom soup, sour cream, green chiles and water in a large bowl and mix well. Stir into the beef mixture.

Layer half the tortilla pieces in a 9×13-inch pan coated with nonstick cooking spray. Top with half the meat mixture and then sprinkle with cheese. Repeat the layers. Bake at 350 degrees for 30 to 35 minutes or until the cheese is melted and the pie is bubbly in the center. Serve with salad and tortilla chips.

*Jayne and Dennis Wayne*

# BISCUIT TACO CUPS

1 1/2 pounds lean ground beef
1 (15-ounce) can spicy
  chili beans
1 envelope taco seasoning mix
1/2 cup water
1 (8-count) can
  refrigerator biscuits

1 cup (4 ounces) shredded
  Cheddar cheese
1/2 cup shredded lettuce
1/2 cup chopped tomato
1/2 cup sour cream
1/2 cup salsa

Brown the ground beef in a skillet over medium-high heat, stirring until crumbly; drain. Add the beans, seasoning mix and water to the ground beef in the skillet and mix well. Reduce the heat to medium and simmer for 10 minutes or until the mixture is slightly thickened, stirring occasionally.

Coat the outside surfaces of eight (6-ounce) custard cups with nonstick cooking spray. Separate the biscuit dough and pat or roll each biscuit into a 4 1/2-inch circle on a lightly floured surface. Place over the outside of the inverted custard cups and press to fit over the bottoms and part of the way down the sides. Place the cups upside down in a 10×15-inch baking pan. Bake at 375 degrees for 14 to 16 minutes or until deep golden brown. Remove the biscuit cups from the custard cups carefully. Place right side up on a serving dish. Spoon the ground beef mixture evenly into each cup. Top evenly with the cheese, lettuce, tomato, sour cream and salsa.

*Kathy Orwig*

# CHRISTMAS EVE MEATBALLS

1 (38-ounce) package frozen meatballs
1 (12-ounce) bottle chili sauce
1 (12-ounce) jar grape jelly

Bake the meatballs according to the package directions; drain.
Combine the chili sauce and grape jelly in a slow cooker and cook
on Low until heated through. Stir the meatballs into the sauce
and keep warm.

*Becky James*


# SAUSAGE ROLLS

2 (8-count) cans refrigerator crescent rolls
1 pound bulk pork sausage

Unroll the roll dough on waxed paper. Shape into a large rectangle,
pressing the perforations to seal. Spread the sausage thinly over
the dough. Roll as for a jelly roll, sealing the edge and ends. Wrap in
waxed paper and chill for 2 hours. Unwrap and then cut into
1/2-inch slices. Place on a baking sheet and bake at 375 degrees for
8 to 10 minutes or until golden brown.

*Chris Sale*

# CHEESE AND OLIVE BALLS

2 cups all-purpose flour
2 cups (8 ounces) shredded Cheddar cheese
1 cup (2 sticks) butter, melted
Olives

Combine the flour and cheese in a bowl. Stir in the butter until the mixture is the consistency of dough. Pat the dough by teaspoonfuls into circles on a lightly floured surface. Drain olives on a paper towel. Place one olive in the center of each circle. Fold the dough around the olive and shape into a ball to enclose. Place on a baking sheet. Bake at 350 degrees for 12 to 15 minutes or until brown.

*Jayne and Dennis Davis*

# EASY MUSHROOM CRESCENT SNACKS

3 cups finely chopped
   fresh mushrooms
2 tablespoons (or less) butter
1/2 teaspoon garlic salt
2 tablespoons finely chopped
   onion, or 1/2 teaspoon dried
   minced onion
1 teaspoon lemon juice

1 teaspoon
   Worcestershire sauce
1 (8-count) can refrigerator
   crescent rolls
3 ounces cream
   cheese, softened
1/4 cup (1 ounce) grated
   Parmesan cheese

Sauté the mushrooms in the butter in a skillet over medium heat until tender. Stir in the garlic salt, onion, lemon juice and Worcestershire sauce. Cook over medium heat until the liquid evaporates.

Unroll the dough and separate into two rectangles. Press over the bottom and up the sides of a 9×13-inch baking pan. Spread the cream cheese over the dough. Spoon the mushroom mixture evenly over the cream cheese. Sprinkle with the Parmesan cheese. Bake at 350 degrees for 20 to 25 minutes or until golden brown. Cool in the pan for 5 minutes. Cut into rectangles and serve warm.

These snacks can be prepared ahead of time and refrigerated for up to 2 hours before baking. Refrigerate any leftovers; to reheat, wrap in foil and bake at 350 degrees for 8 to 10 minutes.

*Kimberly Stanton Bowe*

# BAKED COUSCOUS AND SPINACH APPETIZER

1 1/2 cups boiling water
1 cup couscous
1/2 teaspoon salt
3 garlic cloves, minced
1 large onion,
  finely chopped
1/4 cup olive oil
1 (28-ounce) can
  diced tomatoes

1 1/2 tablespoons fresh basil, or
  1 teaspoon dried basil
1/3 cup pine nuts, chopped
5 cups loosely packed fresh
  spinach, trimmed and torn
  into small pieces
Pepper to taste
2 cups (8 ounces) shredded
  Muenster cheese

Pour the boiling water over the couscous in a heatproof bowl and mix well. Stir in the salt. Cover and let stand for 5 minutes. Fluff with a fork. Sauté the garlic and onion in the olive oil in a large skillet over medium heat for 10 minutes or until tender. Add the tomatoes and cook for 10 minutes, stirring frequently. Stir the tomato mixture into the couscous. Add the basil, pine nuts, spinach and pepper and mix well. Layer the couscous mixture and cheese one-half at a time in a 2 1/2-quart baking dish, ending with the cheese. Cover and bake at 375 degrees for 25 minutes or until hot and bubbly. Serve with French bread or crackers.

*Janet Warren*

# CORNED BEEF DIP IN HAWAIIAN BREAD BOWL

2 cups sour cream
1 1/3 cups mayonnaise
2 teaspoons minced onion
1 teaspoon dill weed
2 teaspoons Beau Monde seasoning
3 tablespoons parsley
3 (4-ounce) packages thinly sliced
   corned beef, torn
1 round loaf Hawaiian bread

Combine the sour cream, mayonnaise, onion, dill weed, Beau Monde seasoning and parsley in a large bowl and mix well. Stir in the corned beef. Cover and chill thoroughly in the refrigerator.

Slice off the top of the bread. Cut chunks of bread out of the center, leaving the outer wall of the loaf and reserving the bread chunks. Fill the center with the dip. Place the bread bowl on a serving platter and surround with the reserved bread chunks and fresh vegetables for dipping.

*Roger Harmon*

# BUFFALO CHICKEN DIP

2 (10-ounce) cans chunk chicken, drained
3/4 cup hot red pepper sauce
16 ounces cream cheese, softened
1 cup ranch salad dressing
1 1/2 cups (6 ounces) shredded Cheddar cheese
1 bunch celery, cut into 4-inch sticks
Crackers

Heat the chicken and hot sauce in a skillet over medium heat until heated through. Stir in the cream cheese and salad dressing. Cook until heated through, stirring constantly. Stir in one-half of the Cheddar cheese. Spoon into a slow cooker and sprinkle the remaining Cheddar cheese over the top. Cover and cook on Low until hot and bubbly. Serve with celery sticks and crackers.

*Pam Hite*

# Black Bean Dip

1 onion, chopped
1 jalapeño chile, finely chopped (optional)
1 green bell pepper, chopped
2 teaspoons olive oil
1 (16-ounce) cans diced tomatoes
1 (16-ounce) can black beans, drained and rinsed
1 (16-ounce) can sweet whole kernel corn, drained
1 (15-ounce) can pineapple tidbits, drained
1 (8-ounce) can peaches, drained and chopped (optional)
1/2 cup shredded chicken (optional)
1/4 cup chopped fresh cilantro
1 avocado, chopped
Shredded cheese

Sauté the onion, jalapeño chile and bell pepper in the olive oil in a skillet over medium heat until tender. Combine the tomatoes, beans, corn, pineapple, peaches and chicken in a large saucepan. Cook over medium-low heat for about 20 minutes. Stir in the onion mixture. Add the cilantro and cook for 2 minutes. Spoon into serving bowls and top with the avocado. Sprinkle with cheese and serve.

For a more creamy dip, stir in a small amount of sour cream or mayonnaise before serving.

*Tracy Orwig*

# CRAB SPREAD

1/2 cup plain yogurt or sour cream
2 tablespoons mayonnaise
8 ounces cream cheese or Neufchâtel cheese, softened
1 teaspoon horseradish
1/2 teaspoon dry mustard
1/2 teaspoon Worcestershire sauce
1/4 teaspoon hot red pepper sauce
1 cup (4 ounces) shredded Cheddar cheese
8 ounces crab meat, drained and flaked
Paprika

Blend the yogurt, mayonnaise, cream cheese, horseradish, mustard, Worcestershire sauce and hot sauce in a bowl. Stir in the Cheddar cheese and crab meat. Cover and chill in the refrigerator. Sprinkle with paprika just before serving. Serve as a spread, a dip for vegetables or as a sandwich filling.

*Karen Nelson*

# CRAB DIP

16 ounces cream
  cheese, softened
3 tablespoons mayonnaise
3 tablespoons lemon juice
3 tablespoons
  Worcestershire sauce

Dash of garlic salt
1 small onion, finely chopped
1 (12-ounce) bottle chili sauce
14 ounces crab meat, drained
  and flaked
Chopped parsley

Blend the cream cheese, mayonnaise, lemon juice, Worcestershire sauce and garlic salt in a bowl. Stir in the onion. Spread the cream cheese mixture on a serving plate and pour the chili sauce over the top. Spoon the crab meat over the chili sauce. Sprinkle with parsley.

*Deana Trones*


# SHRIMP DIP

16 ounces cream
  cheese, softened
1 cup mayonnaise
1 teaspoon lemon juice

Chopped green onions to taste
1 (4- to 6-ounce) can tiny
  shrimp, drained

Blend the cream cheese, mayonnaise and lemon juice in a bowl. Stir in green onions. Fold in the shrimp. Cover and refrigerate for up to 12 hours. Do not substitute mayonnaise-type salad dressing for the mayonnaise.

*Kristi Cheek*

# HOT FENNEL CHEESE DIP

4 slices bacon
3 fennel bulbs, upper stalks removed
2 garlic cloves
1 cup mayonnaise
1 cup sour cream
4 ounces blue cheese, crumbled
20 peppercorns, crushed
2 tablespoons shredded Parmesan cheese
2 tablespoons dry bread crumbs

Cook the bacon in a skillet until crisp. Drain the bacon, reserving 1 tablespoon of the drippings in the skillet. Crumble the bacon. Cut a thin slice from the bottom of each fennel bulb. Cut the fennel into halves lengthwise. Remove the core and discard. Cut each half crosswise into very thin slices. Sauté the fennel in the reserved bacon drippings in the skillet over medium heat for about 20 minutes or until tender. Add the garlic and cook for 3 to 5 minutes. Remove from the heat. Stir in the bacon, mayonnaise, sour cream, blue cheese and peppercorns. Spoon into a baking dish. Mix the Parmesan cheese and bread crumbs in a small bowl and sprinkle over the fennel mixture. Bake at 400 degrees for 15 minutes or until heated through and light brown on top. Serve with endive, other vegetables or crackers.

*Janet Warren*

# Corn Dip

1 cup mayonnaise
1 1/2 cups sour cream
2 (8-ounce) cans Mexicorn
1 (4-ounce) can chopped green chiles, drained
2 cups (8 ounces) shredded Cheddar cheese
2 cups (8 ounces) shredded Monterey Jack cheese

Blend the mayonnaise and sour cream in a bowl. Stir in the Mexicorn and green chiles. Spoon into a baking dish. Bake at 350 degrees for 55 minutes. Top with the Cheddar cheese and Monterey Jack cheese. Serve warm with corn chips.

*Jayne and Dennis Wayne*

# Old Spanish Inn Mexican Dip

2 cups mayonnaise
1 tablespoon white vinegar
2 tablespoons paprika
4 teaspoons garlic powder

Combine the mayonnaise, vinegar, paprika and garlic powder in a bowl and mix well. Refrigerate until chilled. Serve with chips.

*Deana Trones*

# SPINACH DIP

1 cup sour cream
1 cup mayonnaise
1 (10-ounce) package frozen chopped spinach,
    thawed and drained
1/2 cup chopped green onions
1 teaspoon lemon juice
1 teaspoon parsley flakes
1 teaspoon Beau Monde seasoning
1/2 teaspoon dill weed
1/2 teaspoon salt

Blend the sour cream and mayonnaise in a bowl. Stir in the spinach, green onions, lemon juice, parsley flakes, Beau Monde seasoning, dill weed and salt. Serve with fresh vegetables.

*Roger Harmon*

# Hummus

2 (15-ounce) cans garbanzo beans, drained and rinsed
1/4 cup tahini
3 tablespoons sesame oil
2 tablespoons (heaping) chopped garlic, or to taste
2 tablespoons lemon juice, or to taste
1/2 cup (about) water
1 tablespoon tapenade, or to taste
Kosher salt to taste

Process the beans, tahini, sesame oil, garlic, lemon juice and 1/4 cup of the water in a blender at high speed until smooth, stopping the blender occasionally to scrape down the sides of the container. With the blender running, add enough of the remaining water to reach the desired consistency. Add the tapenade and salt and process until blended. Spoon into a serving bowl and serve with tortilla chips or fresh vegetables.

*Tracy Orwig*

# ARTICHOKE HUMMUS

1 (15-ounce) can garbanzo beans
1/2 cup canned artichoke hearts
2 tablespoons extra-virgin olive oil
2 garlic cloves, minced
1/4 teaspoon lemon juice
1/8 teaspoon salt
1/8 teaspoon pepper

Process the beans, artichoke hearts, olive oil, garlic, lemon juice, salt
and pepper in a blender at high speed until smooth, stopping
the blender occasionally to scrape down the sides of the container.
Spoon into a serving bowl. Serve with wedges of pita bread or
fresh vegetables such as steamed fresh asparagus spears, sugar snap
peas and baby carrots.

*Tracy Orwig*

# BLACK BEAN HUMMUS

1 (15-ounce) can black beans
1 garlic clove
2 tablespoons lemon juice
1 1/2 tablespoons tahini
1/2 to 3/4 teaspoon cumin
1/2 teaspoon salt
1/8 to 1/4 teaspoon cayenne pepper
1/4 teaspoon paprika
10 Greek olives

Drain the beans, reserving the liquid. Mince the garlic in a food processor by pulsing four or five times. Add the black beans and 2 tablespoons of the reserved liquid; pulse to combine. Add the lemon juice, tahini, cumin, salt and cayenne pepper and process until smooth, stopping the processor and scraping the inside of the bowl as needed. Add additional reserved liquid to taste. Spoon into a serving bowl and sprinkle with the paprika. Top with the olives.

*Tracy Orwig*

# Frijole Hummus

1 (15-ounce) can black beans or pinto beans, drained
2 tablespoons tahini
1 garlic clove, minced
1 tablespoon lemon juice
1 tablespoon olive oil
$^1/_2$ teaspoon cumin
Salt to taste

Combine the beans, tahini, garlic, lemon juice, olive oil, cumin and salt in a food processor and process until smooth. Spoon into a serving bowl and serve with pita chips, wedges of warm pita bread or tortilla chips.

*Dawn Chaffee*

# HOMEMADE CHEX MIX

10 cups Cheerios
8 cups corn Chex
4 cups bran Chex
3 cups pecan halves and/or other nuts
1/2 cup (1 stick) butter, melted
1/4 cup olive oil
2 teaspoons garlic powder
1 1/2 teaspoons sea salt or seasoning salt
1/2 teaspoon onion powder
1/2 teaspoon Louisiana Hot Sauce or Tabasco sauce

Stir together the Cheerios, corn Chex and bran Chex in a large
bowl. Mix the butter, olive oil, garlic powder, sea salt, onion powder
and hot sauce in a small bowl. Pour over the cereal mixture and
toss until coated. Place in a baking pan. Bake at 250 degrees for
40 minutes, tossing once after 20 minutes of baking.

*Jessica Murray*

# Mint Tea

1 cup mint leaves, rinsed in cold water
1 gallon hot brewed caffeine-free tea
1 cup raw sugar
1 cup lemon juice

Stir the mint leaves into the hot tea and let stand for 30 minutes.
Add the sugar and stir to dissolve. Stir in the lemon juice. Pour into
ice-filled glasses and garnish with sprigs of mint. You may substitute
2 cups fresh lemonade for the lemon juice.

*Deana Trones*

# WATERMELON RASPBERRY SLUSH

4 cups chopped seeded watermelon
3/4 cup soft vanilla ice cream or frozen yogurt
1 tablespoon honey
1/2 cup raspberries
2 teaspoons lemon juice

Spread the watermelon over a baking sheet lined with waxed paper. Freeze for 45 minutes or until firm. Process the ice cream, honey, raspberries and lemon juice in a blender until smooth. Add the frozen watermelon and process until slushy. Pour into a pitcher or glasses.

*Pamela Hathaway*

# SOUPS
## &
## SALADS

# Taco Soup

1 pound ground round
1 small onion, chopped
1 (4-ounce) can chopped green chiles
1 envelope taco seasoning mix
1 envelope ranch salad dressing mix
1 teaspoon salt
1 (14-ounce) can hominy
3 (14-ounce) cans stewed tomatoes
1 (15-ounce) can kidney beans
1 (15-ounce) can pinto beans
1 1/2 cups water

Brown the beef in a skillet, stirring until crumbly; drain. Spoon into a large saucepan or soup pot. Stir in the onion, green chiles, taco seasoning mix, salad dressing mix and salt. Add the hominy, tomatoes, kidney beans, pinto beans and water and mix well. Bring to a boil and reduce the heat. Simmer for 30 to 40 minutes or until heated through. Ladle into serving bowls and serve with cornbread or crackers.

*Nan Yancey*

# TORTILLA SOUP

2 or 3 boneless skinless
  chicken breasts
1 green bell pepper, chopped
1 tomato, chopped
1/2 yellow onion, chopped
1/2 cup tomato sauce
1/4 cup chicken consommé
2 tablespoons granulated garlic
Pinch of dark chili powder

1 tablespoon white pepper
1 tablespoon salt
20 cilantro leaves
8 corn tortillas
Vegetable oil
2 or 3 avocados, sliced
1 1/2 cups (6 ounces) shredded
  Monterey Jack cheese
Additional cilantro

Boil the chicken in water to cover in a saucepan until cooked through.
Remove the chicken from the saucepan and chop, reserving 4 cups
of the broth in the saucepan. Stir the bell pepper, tomato, onion and
tomato sauce into the reserved broth. Add the chicken consommé,
garlic, chili powder, white pepper and salt and mix well. Stir in the
chicken and 20 cilantro leaves. Bring to a boil and reduce the heat
to medium. Simmer for 30 to 45 minutes or until the vegetables
are tender. Longer cooking time enhances the flavor. Cut the tortillas
into strips and fry in a small amount of oil in a skillet until crisp.
Ladle the soup into serving bowls. Top evenly with the avocados,
cheese, tortilla strips and additional cilantro.

*Jennifer Dixon*

# BLACK-EYED PEA SOUP

1 pound hot bulk pork sausage
1 onion, chopped
1 teaspoon chopped garlic
2 (15-ounce) cans black-eyed peas
1 (16-ounce) can tomatoes
1 teaspoon chili powder
Cayenne pepper to taste

Brown the sausage in a skillet, stirring until crumbly; drain. Add the onion and garlic and sauté over medium heat for 5 minutes or until the vegetables are tender. Spoon into a large saucepan. Stir in the peas, tomatoes, chili powder and cayenne pepper. Bring to a boil and reduce the heat to medium. Simmer for 1 hour.

*Kristi Cheek*

# SPICY SHRIMP CHOWDER

1 small onion, chopped
Butter
2 (10-ounce) cans potato soup
2 soup cans of milk
1 (15-ounce) can whole-kernel corn, drained
8 ounces cream cheese, cubed
Minced jalapeño chiles, to taste
1 cup frozen small shrimp

Sauté the onion in a small amount of butter in a saucepan until tender. Stir in the soup, milk and corn. Add the cream cheese and cook over medium heat until melted, stirring frequently. Stir in jalapeño chiles and the shrimp. Cook until the shrimp turn pink. Ladle into soup bowls and garnish with paprika and Parmesan crisps. This soup is even better reheated.

*Kristi Cheek*

# CHUNKY MINESTRONE

1 onion, chopped
2 carrots, sliced
1 3/4 teaspoons olive oil
1 tablespoon chopped garlic
1 (28-ounce) can
  diced tomatoes
2 (10-ounce) cans chicken broth
1 cup water
1/2 cup rice
1 teaspoon basil
1 teaspoon oregano

1 teaspoon thyme
1 teaspoon pepper
1 (19-ounce) can cannellini
1 (10-ounce) package frozen
  chopped spinach, thawed
  and drained
1 zucchini, cut into halves
  and sliced
Salt and pepper to taste
Shredded Parmesan cheese

Sauté the onion and carrots in the hot olive oil in a saucepan over medium heat for 3 minutes. Add the garlic and sauté for 2 minutes. Stir in the tomatoes, chicken broth, water, rice, basil, oregano, thyme and 1 teaspoon pepper. Bring to a boil. Reduce the heat and simmer for 20 minutes. Stir in the beans, spinach, zucchini, salt and pepper to taste. Cook for 5 minutes or until heated through. Ladle into soup bowls and sprinkle with Parmesan cheese.

*Janet Warren*

# CHEESE SOUP

1 small head cabbage, chopped
1 cup chopped celery
1 cup chopped carrots
1 small onion, chopped
1/2 cup (1 stick) margarine,
  melted

8 cups water
5 chicken bouillon cubes
2 potatoes (or more), peeled
  and chopped
12 ounces Velveeta
  cheese, cubed

Sauté the cabbage, celery, carrots and onion in the margarine in
a large saucepan over medium heat. Add the water and bouillon
cubes, stirring until the bouillon cubes are dissolved. Stir in the
potatoes. Reduce the heat to low and simmer for 1 hour. Add the
cheese and simmer for 30 minutes, stirring occasionally.

*Jeanie Seale*

# TOMATO BASIL SOUP

8 to 10 tomatoes, peeled,
  cored and chopped
4 cups tomato juice or
  chicken stock

12 to 14 basil leaves
1 cup heavy cream
1/2 cup (1 stick) butter
1/4 teaspoon cracked pepper

Combine the tomatoes and tomato juice in a saucepan. Bring to
a boil and then reduce the heat. Simmer for 30 minutes. Combine
the tomato mixture and basil in a food processor and process until
smooth. Return the mixture to the saucepan and add the cream,
butter and pepper. Cook over low heat until blended and heated
through, stirring constantly.

*Jessica Murray*

# GREEK SALAD

1 bag Italian salad greens
1 bunch green onions, chopped
1 cup frozen green peas, thawed
1 (3-ounce) jar sliced green olives, drained
1 large cucumber, peeled, cut into quarters and sliced
8 ounces crumbled feta cheese
1/3 cup olive oil
3 tablespoons honey
1 tablespoon lemon juice
1 teaspoon minced garlic
1 large avocado, sliced

Toss the salad greens, green onions, peas, olives, cucumber and cheese together in a large salad bowl. Whisk the olive oil, honey, lemon juice and garlic in a small bowl until well blended. Pour over the salad and toss to coat. Top with the avocado.

*Janet Warren*

# ARMANDO SALAD

1/4 cup sour cream
1/4 cup olive oil
2 tablespoons wine vinegar
1 egg, beaten
Juice of 1 lime
2 tablespoons chopped anchovies
2 teaspoons crumbled crisp-cooked bacon
3/4 garlic clove, minced
1 teaspoon salad herbs
Salt and pepper to taste
Romaine, torn into pieces
Parmesan cheese
Parsley flakes
Croutons

Whisk the sour cream, olive oil, vinegar, egg and lime juice in
a small bowl until the olive oil and egg are incorporated. Stir in
the anchovies, bacon, garlic, salad herbs, salt and pepper. Pour
the dressing over romaine in a bowl and toss to coat. Top with
Parmesan cheese, parsley and croutons.

If you are concerned about using raw eggs, use eggs pasteurized
in their shells, which are sold at some specialty food stores, or
use an equivalent amount of pasteurized egg substitute.

*Leslye Floyd*

# SEVEN-LAYER SALAD

Lettuce, torn into pieces
1 red onion, sliced
1 green bell pepper, sliced
Broccoli florets
Sliced carrots
1 (10-ounce) package frozen peas, thawed
Mayonnaise-type salad dressing
$1/2$ envelope artificial sweetener
Tomato wedges or chopped tomatoes
Shredded Cheddar cheese

Layer lettuce, onion, bell pepper, broccoli, carrots and peas in a large glass salad bowl. Spread the salad dressing over the top in a thick layer, sealing to the edge. Sprinkle with the artificial sweetener. Chill for 10 to 12 hours to allow the flavors to blend. Top with tomatoes and cheese. Spoon through all the layers when serving.

*Carolyn Hardin*

# SEVEN-LAYER TACO SALAD

Shredded lettuce
Chopped onion
Chopped tomato
2 or 3 (14-ounce) cans kidney, chili or black beans, drained
1 bag nacho cheese-flavored tortilla chips, crumbled
Creamy Italian salad dressing
Shredded Mexican blend cheese

Layer lettuce, onion, tomato, beans and chips in a large glass or clear plastic salad bowl. Pour salad dressing over the top and sprinkle with cheese. Spoon through all the layers when serving.

*Ginger Holley*

# ASIAN SLAW

2 (3-ounce) packages Oriental-flavor ramen noodles
1 (16-ounce) bag coleslaw
1 cup sunflower seed kernels
1 cup slivered almonds
Chopped green onions
3/4 cup vegetable oil
1/2 cup sugar
1/3 cup vinegar

Crumble the noodles, reserving the seasoning packets. Layer the noodles, coleslaw, sunflower seeds, almonds and green onions in a large salad bowl. Whisk the oil, sugar, vinegar and reserved seasoning packets in a small bowl and pour over the salad. Do not toss. Marinate in the refrigerator for 3 to 12 hours. Toss the slaw just before serving. This recipe can be doubled for large groups.

*Shirley Montgomery*

# Texas Panhandle Salad

1 cup sunflower oil or olive oil
1/3 cup seasoned rice vinegar
1/3 cup artificial sweetener
2 (3-ounce) packages chicken-
    flavor ramen noodles
1 cup slivered almonds
1/2 cup sesame seeds
1/4 cup (1/2 stick)
    butter, melted

1 large head (or 2 small heads)
    Napa cabbage, chopped
1 bunch green onions, sliced
1 red bell pepper,
    finely chopped
1 yellow bell pepper,
    finely chopped
1/2 bunch cilantro, chopped
2 or 3 avocados, sliced

Whisk the sunflower oil, vinegar and artificial sweetener in a small bowl until the oil is incorporated. Crumble the ramen noodles, reserving the seasoning packets. Mix the noodles, almonds, sesame seeds and butter in small bowl. Sprinkle with the reserved seasoning packets and toss to mix. Spread the noodle mixture over a 10×16-inch baking sheet and bake at 325 degrees for 15 to 20 minutes or until light brown. Remove from the oven and cool. Combine the cabbage, green onions, bell peppers, and cilantro in a large salad bowl. Before serving, toss the cabbage mixture and the noodle mixture together in the bowl. Whisk the dressing again and add just enough to lightly coat the salad. Top with the avocados before serving.

The dressing can be made in advance and stored in a bottle in the refrigerator. The noodle mixture and the cabbage mixture can also be made several hours in advance and stored separately in large sealable plastic bags in the refrigerator.

*Deana Trones*

# Easy Black Bean and Corn Salad

1 (15-ounce) can whole
    kernel corn
1 (15-ounce) can black beans,
    drained and rinsed
1 (7-ounce) can green chiles
2 tomatoes, chopped

1 yellow onion, chopped
1/4 cup chopped cilantro
2 cloves garlic, minced
2 teaspoons lemon juice
Salt and pepper to taste

Combine the corn, beans, green chiles, tomatoes, onion, cilantro, garlic, lemon juice, salt and pepper in a large bowl and mix well. Serve at room temperature.

*Jessica Murray*


# Tomato Refresher

2 small green bell
    peppers, chopped
2 small onions, chopped
2/3 cup chopped celery
1 cup cold water

1 cup sugar
1/4 cup vinegar
1 tablespoon salt
1/4 teaspoon pepper
1 tomato, sliced

Combine the bell peppers, onions and celery in a bowl. Whisk the water, sugar, vinegar, salt and pepper in a small bowl. Pour over the bell pepper mixture and mix well. Spoon over the tomato slices in a dish. Cover and chill for 3 to 4 hours.

*Kathy Orwig*

# Super Summer Potato Salad

3 pounds red potatoes
1 teaspoon salt
1/4 cup cider vinegar
2 tablespoons Italian parsley, chopped
1/2 teaspoon salt
1/2 teaspoon freshly ground pepper
1 cup chopped celery
1 cup finely chopped sweet onion
1/2 cup finely chopped red bell pepper
1/4 cup chopped sweet pickles
1/4 cup chopped dill pickles
6 hard-cooked eggs
3/4 cup fat-free mayonnaise

Place the potatoes and 1 teaspoon salt in a large saucepan and add water to cover. Bring to a boil over high heat. Reduce the heat to medium-high and cook for 25 to 30 minutes or until the potatoes can be pierced easily with a fork; drain. Gently rub off the potato skins if desired. Cut into 1-inch pieces. Whisk the vinegar, parsley, 1/2 teaspoon salt and the pepper in a small bowl. Pour over the potatoes in a large bowl and toss to coat. Stir in the celery, onion, bell pepper, sweet pickles and dill pickles. Remove the yolks from four of the eggs and discard; chop the remaining eggs. Fold the eggs and mayonnaise into the potato mixture. Cover and chill for 2 to 12 hours.

*Deana Trones*

# TABOULI

1 1/2 cups tabouli mix
1 1/4 cups cold water
Chopped tomato
Chopped cucumber
3 to 4 tablespoons finely chopped mint
1/3 cup olive oil
Juice of 1/2 lemon

Combine the tabouli mix and water in a bowl and mix well. Stir in tomato, cucumber and the mint. Whisk the olive oil and lemon juice in a small bowl until the olive oil is incorporated. Add to the tabouli mixture and mix well. Cover and chill for 2 hours before serving.

*Janet Warren*

# Quinoa and Pecan Salad with Dried Cranberries

3 1/2 cups water
1 1/2 cups quinoa
1 bunch green onions,
  finely sliced
1/3 cup cilantro, finely chopped
3/4 cup finely chopped celery
3/4 cup coarsely chopped
  pecans, toasted

1/2 cup dried
  cranberries, chopped
2 tablespoons fresh lemon juice
1 tablespoon rice wine vinegar
1 tablespoon olive oil
1 tablespoon sesame oil
1/4 teaspoon salt
Pinch of pepper

Bring the water to boil in a saucepan. Stir in the quinoa and reduce the heat to a simmer. Cover and cook for 25 to 30 minutes or until the quinoa is soft and the water is absorbed. Let stand until cool and spoon into a large salad bowl. Stir in the green onions, cilantro, celery, pecans and cranberries. Whisk the lemon juice, vinegar, olive oil, sesame oil, salt and pepper in a small bowl until the olive oil and sesame oil are incorporated. Add to the quinoa mixture and mix well. Let stand for 1 hour to blend the flavors. Serve at room temperature.

*Janet Warren*

# Spinach and Blueberry Salad

1 cup blueberries
1 green onion, minced
$1/2$ cup extra-virgin olive oil
$1/3$ cup raspberry vinegar
$1^1/2$ tablespoons honey
1 teaspoon salt
2 (10-ounce) bags spinach salad mix
1 cup blueberries
$1/2$ cup pecans, toasted and chopped
$1/2$ cup blue cheese, crumbled

Process 1 cup blueberries, the green onion, olive oil, vinegar, honey and salt in a blender until smooth. Combine the spinach, 1 cup blueberries, the pecans and cheese in a large salad bowl. Refrigerate until ready to serve. Pour the dressing over the spinach mixture just before serving and toss to combine.

*Deana Trones*

# SPINACH SALAD WITH STRAWBERRIES

Fresh baby spinach, rinsed and trimmed
Red onion slices
Strawberries, thinly sliced
Pine nuts or sesame seeds
Sweet-and-sour salad dressing

Combine spinach, onion, strawberries and pine nuts in a large salad bowl and toss to mix. Top with sweet-and-sour dressing.

*Marty Gustely*

# Salad Greens with Pears and Gorgonzola

Mixed young salad greens, chilled
2 Comice pears, peeled and cut into small cubes
2 tablespoons Gorgonzola cheese
2 to 3 tablespoons walnut oil
2 to 3 tablespoons balsamic vinegar
Salt and pepper to taste
Toasted walnuts

Combine salad greens with the pears and cheese in a large salad bowl. Whisk the walnut oil, vinegar, salt and pepper in a small bowl until the walnut oil is incorporated. Pour over the salad greens mixture and toss to combine. Sprinkle walnuts over the top.

*Janet Warren*

# CRANBERRY BANANA MOLD

1 (3-ounce) package raspberry gelatin
1 cup boiling water
1 (16-ounce) can whole cranberry sauce
2 bananas, sliced
1/2 cup chopped pecans

Dissolve the gelatin in the boiling water in a heatproof bowl. Stir in the cranberry sauce. Chill until partially set. Fold in the bananas and pecans. Spoon into a mold and chill until firm.

*Linda Hardin*

# LIME GELATIN SALAD

1 (6-ounce) package lime gelatin
2 cups boiling water
8 ounces cottage cheese or cream cheese, softened
1 (8-ounce) can crushed pineapple, drained
Chopped pecans

Dissolve the gelatin in the boiling water in a bowl. Let stand until warm. Stir in the cottage cheese, pineapple and pecans. Pour into a mold and chill until firm. If using cream cheese instead of the cottage cheese, use a mixer to blend it with the gelatin mixture before adding the pineapple and pecans.

*Linda Hardin*

# Asian Chicken Salad

## Asian Dressing

1/4 cup reduced-sodium
   soy sauce
3 tablespoons rice wine vinegar
1 1/2 tablespoons brown sugar
1 1/2 teaspoons sesame oil
1 1/2 teaspoons chile-garlic sauce
1 tablespoon minced
   fresh ginger
2 garlic cloves, minced
3 tablespoons canola oil
3/4 cup reduced-sodium
   chicken broth, or 3/4 cup
   reserved liquid from
   poaching the chicken
1 tablespoon tahini

## Chicken Salad

2 tablespoons sesame seeds
8 cups shredded napa cabbage
   (about 1 small head)
3 1/2 cups shredded cooked
   chicken breasts
   (about 1 1/2 pounds boneless
   skinless chicken breasts)
1 1/2 cups grated carrots
   (2 to 3 carrots)
5 radishes, sliced
1/2 cup chopped scallions

To prepare the dressing, whisk the soy sauce, vinegar, brown sugar, sesame oil and chile-garlic sauce in a small bowl until blended. Sauté the ginger and garlic in the canola oil in a small saucepan over medium-high heat for 1 to 2 minutes or until fragrant. Stir in the soy sauce mixture and bring to a simmer. Whisk in the broth and tahini. Cook over medium-high heat for 3 to 4 minutes or until the liquid is slightly reduced, stirring frequently. Let cool.

To prepare the salad, toast the sesame seeds in a small skillet over medium-low heat for 1 to 2 minutes or until light brown and fragrant, stirring constantly. Remove to a small plate to cool. Combine the cabbage, chicken, carrots, radishes and scallions in a large shallow bowl. Whisk the dressing and then drizzle over the chicken mixture. Toss to coat. Sprinkle the sesame seeds over the top.

*Tracy Westhoff*

# WONDERFUL CHICKEN SALAD

5 boneless skinless chicken breasts, cooked and
coarsely chopped
1 (20-ounce) can crushed pineapple, drained
1 cup halved purple grapes
1 cup chopped pecans
1 apple, peeled, cored and chopped
1/2 cup chopped celery
1 1/2 to 2 cups mayonnaise-type salad dressing
5 garlic cloves, crushed

Combine the chicken, pineapple, grapes, pecans, apple and celery in
a large salad bowl. Mix the salad dressing and garlic in a small bowl.
Spoon into the chicken mixture and mix well. Serve on croissants.

*Jayne and Dennis Davis*

# COCONUT CHICKEN SALAD

4 boneless skinless chicken breasts, cooked and
    coarsely chopped
2 cups chopped celery
2 cups halved red and green grapes
1 (16-ounce) can pineapple tidbits, drained
1 cup chopped pecans
1 cup shredded coconut
1 cup mayonnaise
1 cup sour cream
2 teaspoons salt

Combine the chicken, celery, grapes, pineapple, pecans and coconut
in a large bowl. Blend the mayonnaise, sour cream and salt in a small
bowl. Spoon into the chicken mixture and mix well.

*Tracy Orwig*

# Orange Tarragon Chicken Salad

ORANGE TARRAGON DRESSING
1/2 cup light mayonnaise or
   mayonnaise-type salad dressing
2 tablespoons milk or
   orange juice
1 tablespoon grated orange zest
2 to 3 teaspoons chopped
   fresh tarragon, or
   3/4 teaspoon dried tarragon
2 teaspoons Dijon mustard
1/4 teaspoon salt

CHICKEN SALAD
5 ounces bow tie
   pasta or rotini
2 cups chopped
   cooked chicken
3/4 cup celery
1 (11-ounce) can mandarin
   oranges, drained
1 kiwifruit, peeled and chopped

To prepare the dressing, blend the mayonnaise, milk, orange zest, tarragon, Dijon mustard and salt in a small bowl. Refrigerate while preparing the salad.

To prepare the salad, cook the pasta using the package directions; drain and rinse with cold water. Let stand until cool. Combine the pasta, chicken, celery and mandarin oranges in a large bowl. Pour the dressing over the chicken mixture and toss gently to coat. Cover and refrigerate until ready to serve. Add the kiwifruit and toss gently just before serving.

You may use basil instead of the tarragon.

*Kathy Orwig*

# TORTELLINI SALAD

FRENCH DRESSING
$1/3$ cup ketchup
3 tablespoons sugar
3 tablespoons vegetable oil
2 tablespoons vinegar
$1/4$ teaspoon onion powder
$1/4$ teaspoon salt

SALAD
1 (9-ounce) package
refrigerator cheese-filled
tortellini

2 cups shredded lettuce
1 tomato, chopped
$1/4$ cup chopped green onions
2 ounces cooked ham, cut into
thin strips (about $1/3$ cup)
2 ounces cooked turkey,
cut into thin strips
(about $1/3$ cup)
2 hard-cooked eggs, sliced

To prepare the dressing, whisk the ketchup, sugar, oil, vinegar, onion powder and salt in a small bowl until smooth. Refrigerate while preparing the salad.

To prepare the salad, cook the tortellini using the package directions; drain and rinse with cold water. Let stand until cool. Combine the tortellini, lettuce, tomato and green onions in a large bowl and toss to mix. Spoon onto a serving platter. Arrange the ham, turkey and eggs over the salad. Serve with the dressing.

*Kathy Orwig*

# Honey Mustard Salad Dressing

1/4 cup extra-virgin olive oil
2 tablespoons balsamic vinegar
1 tablespoon honey
1 teaspoon Dijon mustard
1/4 teaspoon freshly ground pepper

Whisk the olive oil, vinegar, honey, Dijon mustard and pepper in a small bowl until the olive oil is incorporated. Serve as a salad dressing with salad greens, dried cranberries, walnuts and feta cheese.

This recipe also makes a great marinade for fish or chicken.

*Kristi Cheek*


# Fruit Salad Syrup

1/2 cup balsamic vinegar
1/4 cup water
1/4 cup sugar
Fresh mint leaves, minced

Combine the vinegar, water and sugar in a small saucepan. Bring to a simmer. Stir in the mint. Cook for 12 minutes or until thickened, stirring frequently. Remove from the heat and strain. Let stand until cool. Serve over fresh fruit such as watermelon, pears, cantaloupe and strawberries. Garnish with additional mint leaves.

*Kristi Cheek*

# VEGETABLES
### &
# SIDES

# Bacon-Wrapped Asparagus

1 1/2 pounds asparagus
Extra-virgin olive oil or nonstick cooking spray
Few dashes of salt, or to taste
Freshly ground pepper to taste
4 slices center-cut bacon or pancetta
Fresh lemon juice

Snap off the woody ends of the asparagus spears. Cut the asparagus into 4- to 5-inch pieces. Drizzle with the olive oil in a bowl to lightly coat. Season with salt and pepper. Gather one-fourth of the spears into a bundle and wrap with one slice of the bacon. Secure with a wooden pick. Sprinkle with lemon juice. Repeat with the remaining spears and bacon slices to make four bundles. Place on a grill rack. Grill, covered, over hot coals for 10 to 12 minutes or until the bacon is crisp and the asparagus is tender. To bake in the oven, place the bundles on a rack in a broiler pan. Bake at 400 degrees for 12 minutes.

*Joni Shaw*

# ASPARAGUS AND TOMATOES WITH ALMONDS

2 pounds asparagus
1 tablespoon minced garlic
1 tablespoon butter, melted
1 tablespoon olive oil
10 ounces grape tomatoes or cherry tomatoes,
    cut into halves
Salt and pepper to taste
1 tablespoon lemon juice
3/4 cup slivered almonds, toasted

Snap off the woody ends of the asparagus spears. Cut into 2-inch pieces. Cook in boiling water to cover in a saucepan for 3 minutes. Drain and plunge into a bowl of ice water to stop the cooking process. Sauté the garlic in the butter and olive oil in a skillet over medium heat for 2 minutes. Add the asparagus and tomatoes and sauté for 3 to 5 minutes. Spoon into a serving dish. Season with salt and pepper and toss with the lemon juice. Serve immediately or chill before serving. Sprinkle with the almonds before serving.

*Janet Warren*

# Broccoli and Artichoke Bake

3 (10-ounce) packages frozen broccoli
1 (14-ounce) can artichoke hearts, drained
1 (8-ounce) can mushrooms, drained
2 (8-ounce) rolls garlic cheese, cut into pieces
1 (10-ounce) can cream of mushroom soup
Salt and pepper to taste

Cook the broccoli using the package directions; drain. Combine the broccoli, artichokes, mushrooms, cheese, soup, salt and pepper in a large bowl and mix well. Spoon into a baking dish. Bake at 350 degrees until golden brown and bubbly.

*Chris Sale*

# Broccoli and Rice Casserole

1 tablespoon chopped onion
2 tablespoons butter
1 (10-ounce) package frozen chopped broccoli
1 (10-ounce) can cream of chicken soup or
  cream of mushroom soup
1 (8-ounce) jar Cheez Whiz
1 cup quick-cooking rice

Sauté the onion in the butter in a skillet over medium heat until tender. Add the frozen broccoli and cook just until the broccoli thaws, stirring constantly. Stir in the soup, Cheez Whiz and rice. Spoon into a greased casserole. Bake at 350 degrees for 25 to 35 minutes or until bubbly.

*Lois Clerihew*

# RED PEPPER BROCCOLI

1 bunch broccoli, cut into bite-size pieces
2 garlic cloves, minced
2 tablespoons olive oil
1 or 2 dashes of red pepper flakes
Grated Parmesan cheese

Steam the broccoli on a rack in a steamer until tender-crisp.
Sauté the garlic in the olive oil in a skillet for 2 to 3 minutes.
Add the broccoli and red pepper flakes. Sauté for 3 to 5 minutes
or until the broccoli is tender. Spoon into a serving dish and
sprinkle with cheese.

*Joni Shaw Smith*

# CHEESY BAKED CARROTS

5 cups cooked sliced carrots
8 ounces sliced Velveeta cheese
Salt and pepper to taste
1 small onion, chopped

1/2 cup (1 stick) butter
  or margarine, melted
Butter crackers, crushed

Layer the carrots and cheese in a baking dish. Season with salt and pepper. Sauté the onion in the butter in a skillet over medium heat until tender. Spoon the onion mixture over the prepared layers and top with the crackers. Bake at 350 degrees for 30 minutes.

*Pam Hite*


# CHEESY CORN AND GREEN CHILE BAKE

1 (16-ounce) can
  cream-style corn
1 cup baking mix
1/2 cup milk
2 tablespoons vegetable oil

1 egg, beaten
6 ounces) Monterey Jack
  cheese, shredded
1 (4-ounce) can chopped green
  chiles, drained

Combine the corn, baking mix, milk, oil and egg in a bowl and mix well. Spread one-half of the corn mixture in an 8×8-inch baking dish. Sprinkle the cheese and chiles over the corn mixture. Spread the remaining corn mixture over the top. Bake at 400 degrees for 30 minutes or until the top is golden brown.

*Traci Rutledge*

# Uncle Leonard's Fried Corn

5 slices bacon
3 (15-ounce) cans whole kernel corn, drained
1 (14-ounce) can cream-style corn
1/4 cup (1/2 stick) butter
1 teaspoon sugar
Pepper to taste

Cook the bacon in a skillet until crisp; drain, reserving the drippings in the skillet. Remove the bacon to a plate. Sauté the whole kernel corn in the reserved drippings until crisp. Stir in the cream-style corn, butter, sugar and pepper. Cook over medium heat until heated through, stirring frequently. Spoon into a serving dish. Crumble the bacon over the top.

*Nikki Davis*

# BAKED FENNEL

3 fennel bulbs
1 tablespoon olive oil
1 cup whole wheat bread crumbs
1 garlic clove, chopped
1 tablespoon olive oil
Salt and pepper to taste
Grated Parmesan cheese

Trim the fennel bulbs and cut into quarters lengthwise. Cook in boiling water in a saucepan for 10 minutes or until tender; drain. Place in a baking dish and brush with 1 tablespoon olive oil. Mix the bread crumbs, garlic and 1 tablespoon olive oil in a small bowl; sprinkle over the fennel. Season with salt and pepper. Bake at 375 degrees for 30 minutes or until the bread crumbs are golden brown. Sprinkle with cheese.

*Janet Warren*

# TWICE-BAKED POTATOES

6 to 8 baking potatoes
$1/2$ cup (1 stick) margarine, softened
1 (5-ounce) can evaporated milk
Salt and pepper to taste
1 envelope onion soup mix
Shredded cheese

Scrub the potatoes and pierce with a fork. Place directly on the oven rack and bake at 400 degrees for $1 1/4$ hours or until tender. Remove to a baking sheet and cool for 5 minutes. Cut into halves lengthwise. Scoop the pulp from the potatoes into a mixing bowl, reserving the potato shells. Add the margarine, evaporated milk, salt and pepper to the potato pulp and beat until smooth. (The potato mixture will be thick.) Stir in the soup mix. Spoon the mixture into the reserved potato shells and top with cheese. Bake at 400 degrees for 15 minutes or until the potatoes are heated through and the cheese is melted.

*Linda Hardin*

# DREAMY CREAMY TWICE-BAKED POTATOES

4 large russet potatoes
Coarse salt
1/2 cup (1 stick) butter, softened
4 ounces cream cheese, softened
1/2 cup milk
Salt and pepper to taste
1 1/2 cups (6 ounces) shredded Cheddar cheese
1/2 cup chopped chives
1/2 cup crumbled crisp-cooked bacon

Scrub the potatoes and pierce several times with a fork. Sprinkle coarse salt on a plate and roll the potatoes in the coarse salt. Place the potatoes directly on the oven rack. Bake at 400 degrees for 1 hour or until tender. Remove to a baking sheet and cool for 5 minutes. Cut into halves lengthwise. Scoop the potato pulp into a large mixing bowl, reserving the potato shells. Add the butter, cream cheese, milk, salt and pepper to the potato pulp and beat until smooth. Fold in the Cheddar cheese, chives and bacon. Spoon the mixture into the reserved potato shells. Bake at 400 degrees for 10 to 15 minutes or until the tops are light brown.

*Jessica Murray*

# CREAMY MASHED POTATOES

8 large potatoes, peeled and quartered
1 1/2 cups (or more) milk
8 ounces cream cheese, softened
1 cup sour cream
Salt and pepper to taste
Butter
Paprika to taste
Chopped chives

Cook the potatoes in boiling water in a saucepan until tender; drain. Combine the potatoes, milk, cream cheese and sour cream in a mixing bowl and beat until smooth and fluffy, adding additional milk if necessary. Season with salt and pepper. Spoon into a 9×13-inch baking pan coated with nonstick cooking spray. Dot the top with butter. Bake at 375 degrees for 30 to 40 minutes or until heated through. Sprinkle with paprika and chives. To prepare in advance, spoon the potato mixture into the baking pan and let stand until cool. Cover tightly and refrigerate for up to 24 hours before proceeding as directed above. The mashed potatoes can also be prepared in advance and frozen.

*Kathy Filbert*

# MINIATURE MEATLESS LOAVES

1 cup dry texturized soy protein granules
3/4 cup plus 2 tablespoons boiling water
1 cup tomato sauce
1 cup fork-mashed cooked potatoes
1 cup rolled oats
1 tablespoon dried minced onion
1 teaspoon dried oregano
1/2 teaspoon dry mustard
1/4 teaspoon garlic powder
Salt and pepper to taste

Stir the soy protein granules into the boiling water in a small heat-proof bowl and let stand for 10 minutes. Combine the reconstituted granules, tomato sauce, potatoes and oats in a bowl and mix well. Stir in the onion, oregano, mustard, garlic powder, salt and pepper. Spoon the mixture evenly into eight large greased muffin cups and pack down with the back of a spoon. Bake at 350 degrees for 25 to 30 minutes or until the loaves are light brown and begin to pull away from the sides of the muffin cups. Remove from the oven and let stand for 5 minutes. Invert the loaves onto a serving platter. Serve with ketchup or gravy.

*Janet Warren*

# Rosemary Oven Fries

8 ounces sliced bacon
1 sprig of rosemary
Cracked pepper to taste
2 russet potatoes
1/4 cup extra-virgin olive oil
3/4 teaspoon kosher salt
1/4 cup (1 ounce) freshly grated Parmigiano-Reggiano
2 tablespoons chopped fresh rosemary

Arrange the bacon on a baking sheet. Strip the leaves from the rosemary sprig and sprinkle over the bacon. Sprinkle with pepper. Roast at 400 degrees for 10 minutes or until the bacon is crisp. Remove from the oven.

Increase the oven temperature to 425 degrees. Heat a baking sheet in the oven for at least 5 minutes. Cut the potatoes into halves lengthwise. Cut each half into quarters lengthwise to make sixteen large wedges. Toss the potatoes with the olive oil and kosher salt in a large bowl. Spread the wedges in a single layer on the hot baking sheet. Roast for 30 to 35 minutes or until the potatoes are cooked through, brown and crisp, shaking the baking sheet two or three times while roasting. Remove to a large bowl and toss with the bacon, cheese and 2 tablespoons rosemary.

*Joni Shaw Smith*

# THE BEST POTATOES EVER

1 (32-ounce) package frozen hash brown potatoes, thawed
1 (10-ounce) can creamy chicken verde soup
1 cup sour cream
1/2 cup (1 stick) butter or margarine, melted
2 cups (8 ounces) shredded cheese
1 (3-ounce) can French-fried onions

Combine the potatoes, soup, sour cream and butter in a large
bowl and mix well. Stir in the cheese gradually. Spoon the potato
mixture into a baking dish coated with nonstick cooking spray.
Bake at 350 degrees for 30 to 40 minutes or until heated through.
Top with the onions and bake for 5 more minutes.

This recipe can become a main dish with the addition of more
vegetables or chopped cooked chicken. It can also be prepared with
cream of mushroom soup instead of creamy chicken verde soup.

*Kristi Cheek*

# CORNFLAKE POTATOES

1 (32-ounce) package frozen
   hash brown potatoes, thawed
1 onion, chopped
2 cups (8 ounces) shredded
   Cheddar cheese
2 cups sour cream
1 (10-ounce) can cream of
   chicken soup
1/2 cup (1 stick) butter, melted
1 teaspoon salt
1/4 cup (1/2 stick) butter, melted
3 cups cornflakes

Combine the potatoes, onion, cheese, sour cream, soup, 1/2 cup butter and the salt in a large bowl and mix well. Spoon into a buttered 9×13-inch baking pan. Pour 1/4 cup butter over the cornflakes in a bowl and toss to coat. Sprinkle the cornflakes over the potato mixture. Bake at 350 degrees for 50 minutes.

*Florence Brady Stanton and Mary Kay Brady*

# SWEET POTATO BALLS

4 large sweet potatoes
2/3 cup packed brown sugar
2 tablespoons orange juice
1 teaspoon grated orange zest
1/2 teaspoon freshly grated nutmeg
2 cups sweetened shredded coconut
1/2 cup granulated sugar
1 teaspoon cinnamon
1 (16-ounce) package marshmallows

Bake the sweet potatoes at 350 degrees until tender. Maintain the oven temperature. Let stand until cool enough to handle. Peel the sweet potatoes and mash the pulp in a large bowl. Stir in the brown sugar, orange juice, orange zest and nutmeg. Toss the coconut with the granulated sugar and cinnamon in another bowl. Coat each marshmallow with some of the sweet potato mixture and press to enclose in a 2- to 3-inch diameter ball. Roll the sweet potato balls in the coconut mixture. Place in a baking pan. Bake for 15 to 20 minutes, watching carefully during the last few minutes of baking to make sure the expanding marshmallows do not cause the sweet potato balls to burst.

*Deana Trones*

# SWEET POTATO CUSTARD WITH PECANS

6 large sweet potatoes
3/4 cup granulated sugar
3/4 cup buttermilk
1/2 cup (1 stick) butter, softened
2 eggs, beaten
1 teaspoon baking powder
1 teaspoon vanilla extract
1 teaspoon cinnamon
1 cup packed brown sugar
1/2 cup all-purpose flour
1/3 cup butter, melted
1 cup chopped pecans

Bake the sweet potatoes at 350 degrees until tender. Maintain the oven temperature. Let stand until cool enough to handle. Peel the sweet potatoes and cut the pulp into pieces. Combine the hot sweet potato pulp, granulated sugar, buttermilk, 1/2 cup butter, the eggs, baking powder, vanilla and cinnamon in a mixing bowl and beat until smooth. Spoon the mixture into a buttered 2-quart baking dish. Mix the brown sugar and flour in a small bowl. Add 1/3 cup butter and mix well. Stir in the pecans. Sprinkle over the sweet potato mixture. Bake for 30 minutes or until light brown.

*Margaret Dorland*

# TOMATOES STUFFED WITH PISTACHIOS

4 large tomatoes
1 cup finely chopped onion
2 garlic cloves, minced
2 teaspoons olive oil
1 cup whole wheat bread crumbs
3/4 cup brown rice, cooked
1/2 cup chopped shelled pistachios
Pepper to taste
1 cup vegetable broth or chicken broth

Slice the tops off of the tomatoes. Scoop out the pulp, leaving a 1/4-inch shell. Purée the pulp in a blender. Sauté the onion and garlic in the olive oil in a skillet over medium heat until tender and golden brown. Combine the tomato pulp, onion mixture, bread crumbs, rice, pistachios and pepper in a bowl. Spoon into the tomato shells and place in a baking dish. Pour the broth over the tomatoes. Bake at 345 degrees for about 30 minutes, basting frequently.

*Janet Warren*

# JULIENNED VEGETABLES

12 ounces zucchini, julienned
12 ounces carrots, peeled and julienned
12 ounces yellow squash, julienned
1 tablespoon olive oil
Creole seasoning to taste

Steam the zucchini, carrots and squash on a rack in a steamer or in a double boiler just until tender-crisp. Do not overcook. Toss the vegetables with the olive oil in a serving bowl. Sprinkle with Creole seasoning.

To "julienne" a vegetable means to cut it into long thin strips about 1/4-inch wide.

*Deana Trones*

# MIKE'S SUPER-EASY VEGETABLES

1 large onion or 2 medium onions, thinly sliced
Salt and black pepper to taste
2 zucchini, cut into $1/8$-inch slices
Pinch of cayenne pepper
2 yellow squash, cut into $1/8$-inch slices
Sweet basil to taste
Sliced mushrooms
Lemon pepper to taste
Celery salt to taste
2 Roma tomatoes, sliced
White pepper to taste

Spread the onion over the bottom of a large oiled saucepan. Season with salt and black pepper. Layer the zucchini over the onions. Sprinkle with the cayenne pepper. Layer the yellow squash over the zucchini and sprinkle with basil. Layer the mushrooms over the squash and season with lemon pepper and celery salt. Top with the tomatoes and season with salt and white pepper. Cover the saucepan and cook over high heat for 7 minutes, without stirring. Reduce the heat to medium-high and cook for 5 to 7 minutes, without stirring. Turn off the heat and let stand for 10 minutes before serving.

*Michael Delbridge*

# CREAMY COUSCOUS PARMESAN

1 (5-ounce) box Parmesan couscous
1 cup milk
1 cup fresh spinach, trimmed and torn into pieces
1 teaspoon oregano
1 teaspoon basil
1 cup cherry tomatoes, cut into halves
1 tablespoon lemon juice

Prepare the couscous in a saucepan using the package directions, substituting the milk for the water. Stir in the spinach, oregano and basil. Stir in the tomatoes and lemon juice just before serving.

*Janet Warren*

# Vegetarian Vegetable Couscous

1 onion, chopped
2 garlic cloves, minced
2 tablespoons olive oil
2 teaspoons cumin
1/2 teaspoon turmeric
2 zucchini, cut into
  1/2-inch pieces
1 (16-ounce) can
  diced tomatoes
1 (15-ounce) can chick-peas
  or garbanzo beans, drained
  and rinsed
1/2 cup raisins
1 1/2 cups water
1 cup wheat or
  plain couscous
Grated Parmesan cheese

Sauté the onion and garlic in the olive oil in a saucepan over medium heat for 2 minutes. Add the cumin and turmeric and sauté for 2 minutes. Stir in the zucchini, undrained tomatoes, chick-peas and raisins. Bring to a boil. Reduce the heat to low and simmer for 20 to 30 minutes, stirring occasionally.

Bring the water to a boil in a small saucepan over medium-high heat. Stir in the couscous with a fork. Remove from the heat and let stand for 5 to 10 minutes. Fluff with a fork.

Spoon the couscous into a serving bowl and top with the zucchini mixture. Sprinkle with cheese. Serve as a side dish with chicken or fish.

*Janet Warren*

# BLACK BELUGA LENTIL PILAF

1/2 cup chopped onion
1 to 2 tablespoons olive oil
1 or 2 garlic cloves, minced
1 teaspoon cumin seeds
1 3/4 cups chicken broth or vegetable broth
1 cup basmati rice
1 tablespoon dried currants
1 (15-ounce) can black beluga lentils

Sauté the onion in the olive oil in a saucepan over medium heat for 10 minutes or until tender. Add the garlic and cumin and sauté for 1 minute. Stir in the broth, rice and currants. Bring to a boil. Cover and cook over medium heat for 15 to 20 minutes or until just before the liquid is completely absorbed. Stir in the lentils and cook for 5 minutes. Spoon into a serving bowl.

*Janet Warren*

# GREEK PASTA TOSS

16 ounces penne
1 (14-ounce) can marinated artichoke hearts
2 zucchini, sliced
3 cups sliced mushrooms
1 (4-ounce) can black olives
3/4 cup crumbled feta cheese

Cook the pasta using the package directions; drain and keep warm.
Drain the artichoke hearts, reserving the marinade. Sauté the zucchini
and mushrooms in the reserved marinade in a skillet over medium
heat until the vegetables are tender and light brown. Chop the
artichoke hearts and add to the zucchini mixture. Stir in the olives
and cheese. Cook until heated through, stirring frequently. Spoon into
a serving bowl and toss with the pasta. Serve warm.

This recipe is simple and quick to prepare, but it makes an
elegant dish.

*Karen Nelson*

# HOMEMADE MACARONI AND CHEESE

16 ounces elbow macaroni, cooked and drained
1/4 cup (1/2 stick) butter, softened
2 cups milk
4 eggs, beaten
2 tablespoons Worcestershire sauce
Salt and pepper to taste
4 cups (16 ounces) shredded Cheddar cheese

Spoon the macaroni into a large bowl. Add the butter and stir to coat. Spoon into a 9×13-inch baking pan. Whisk the milk, eggs, Worcestershire sauce, salt and pepper in a bowl and pour over the macaroni. Top with the cheese. Cover with foil and bake at 325 degrees for 30 minutes.

*Joni Shaw Smith*

# Macaroni and Cheese Casserole

2 (15-ounce) cans whole kernel corn, drained
2 (14-ounce) cans cream-style corn
3 cups chopped Velveeta cheese
2 cups macaroni
1 cup (2 sticks) butter, melted
1 green bell pepper, chopped
1 onion, chopped
1/2 teaspoon salt
1/2 teaspoon pepper

Combine the whole kernel corn, cream-style corn, cheese and macaroni in a large bowl and mix well. Pour the butter over the macaroni mixture and mix well. Stir in the bell pepper, onion, salt and pepper. Spoon into a baking dish. Cover and bake at 350 degrees for 40 minutes. Uncover and bake for 15 minutes longer.

*Jayne and Dennis Davis*

# CHINESE-STYLE RICE

1 egg, beaten
1 teaspoon vegetable oil
3/4 cup water
1/4 cup chopped scallions or onion
4 teaspoons soy sauce
1/8 teaspoon garlic salt
1 cup quick-cooking rice

Scramble the egg in the oil in a saucepan over medium heat until no visible raw egg remains, stirring to break into small pieces. Stir in the water, scallions, soy sauce and garlic salt. Bring to a boil and then stir in the rice. Remove from the heat. Cover and let stand for 5 minutes. Spoon into a serving bowl and fluff with a fork.

*Roger Harmon*

# DIRTY RICE

3 onions, chopped
2 or 3 ribs celery, chopped
Minced garlic to taste
Vegetable oil
4 pounds hot bulk pork sausage
Chicken broth
4 cups (or more) cooked rice
Salt to taste
Chopped green onions

Sauté the onions, celery and garlic in a small amount of vegetable oil in a skillet over medium heat until tender. Remove to a small bowl. Brown the sausage in the skillet, stirring until crumbly and adding a small amount of chicken broth to keep it from sticking. The sausage should be cooked through and very brown, almost burnt. Drain the sausage and spoon into a large bowl. Add the onion mixture to the sausage and mix well. Fold in the rice gradually; there should be more sausage mixture than rice in the finished dish. Taste and season with salt if needed. Spoon into a large bowl and sprinkle with green onions.

*Ruth Ann Lisotta*

# BAKED PINEAPPLE

1/2 cup sugar
2 tablespoons cornstarch
1 (29-ounce) can crushed pineapple
4 eggs, beaten
1 teaspoon vanilla extract
2 teaspoons butter, cut into small pieces
1 teaspoon cinnamon

Mix the sugar and cornstarch in a bowl. Add the pineapple and
stir to coat. Stir in the eggs and vanilla. Spoon into a baking dish.
Dot the top with the butter and sprinkle with the cinnamon.
Bake at 350 degrees for 1 hour.

*Marty Gustely*

# MEAT

*&*

# POULTRY

# Beef Burgundy

1 onion, chopped
8 ounces mushrooms, trimmed and sliced
4 garlic cloves, minced
Olive oil
2 pounds sirloin steak, cut into bite-size pieces
$1/2$ teaspoon thyme
$1/2$ teaspoon marjoram
Salt and pepper to taste
$1 1/2$ tablespoons all-purpose flour
2 cups beef consommé
$1 1/2$ cups burgundy
Hot cooked noodles or rice

Sauté the onion, mushrooms and garlic in a small amount of olive oil in a skillet over medium heat until tender. Remove the vegetables from the skillet and reserve. Add a small amount of olive oil and the steak to the skillet and cook until the steak is brown on all sides. Sprinkle with the thyme, marjoram, salt and pepper. Mix the flour and beef consommé in a small bowl and add to the steak in the skillet. Bring to a boil, stirring constantly. Stir in the burgundy. Reduce the heat to low and simmer for 1 hour or until the steak is tender, stirring occasionally. Stir in the reserved onion mixture. Cook until heated through. Spoon over cooked noodles in a serving bowl.

*Leslye Floyd*

# BEEF STEW

3 tablespoons all-purpose flour
1 teaspoon salt
1 1/2 pounds beef stew meat
2 tablespoons vegetable oil
2 cups water or beef broth
2 potatoes, peeled and cut into bite-size pieces
1 large onion, thickly sliced
1 (12-ounce) can diced tomatoes
1 tablespoon minced garlic
1 teaspoon dried thyme
1 1/2 cups sliced carrots

Combine the flour and salt in a sealable plastic bag. Add the beef
a few pieces at a time and shake to coat. Brown the beef in the oil
in a skillet over medium heat. Add the water and stir in the potatoes,
onion, tomatoes, garlic and thyme. Bring to a boil; reduce the heat
to low. Simmer for 1 1/2 hours. Stir in the carrots and simmer for
30 minutes longer. Ladle into serving bowls.

*Janet Warren*

# QUICK BEEF STEW IN BREAD BOWL

1 (11-ounce) can refrigerator French bread
1 (17-ounce) package refrigerator precooked
  beef tips with gravy
1 (9-ounce) package frozen roasted potatoes with
  garlic and herbs
1 (9-ounce) package frozen sweet peas with pearl onions
1/2 cup canned beef gravy
1/3 cup water
1 tablespoon Worcestershire sauce

Cut the French bread dough into quarters. Shape each into a ball, sealing the seams. Place seam side down on a baking sheet coated with nonstick cooking spray. Bake at 350 degrees for 18 to 20 minutes or until deep golden brown. Let stand for 10 minutes to cool.

Microwave the beef tips, potatoes and peas using the package directions for each. Combine the beef tips, potatoes and peas in a microwave-safe 2-quart bowl and mix well. Microwave on High for 1 to 2 minutes or until heated through.

Slice off the tops of the bread loaves. Press gently in the center of each loaf to make a bowl. Place in shallow soup bowls. Ladle the stew into the bread bowls. Serve with the bread tops.

*Kathy Orwig*

# GOOD OLD-FASHIONED CHILI

2 onions, chopped
1 green bell pepper, chopped
2 large ribs celery, chopped
3 garlic cloves, minced
1 jalapeño chile, finely chopped
Vegetable oil
5 pounds lean coarsely ground chuck
1 (15-ounce) can stewed tomatoes
1 (15-ounce) can tomato sauce
12 ounces beer
1 (7-ounce) can chopped green chiles
1 (6-ounce) can tomato paste
6 tablespoons chili powder
Tabasco sauce to taste
3 bay leaves (optional)

Sauté the onions, bell pepper, celery, garlic and jalapeño chile in a small amount of oil in a large saucepan over medium heat until tender. Add the beef and brown, stirring until crumbly; drain. Stir in the tomatoes, tomato sauce, beer, green chiles, tomato paste, chili powder and Tabasco sauce. Add enough water to cover and then stir in the bay leaves. Cook over low heat for 3 hours, stirring every 15 to 20 minutes. Remove and discard the bay leaves before serving. This chili tastes even better reheated.

*Jessica Murray*

# HOME-STYLE GROUND BEEF HASH

1 pound lean ground beef
4 cups frozen hash brown potatoes with onions
1 (11-ounce) can whole kernel corn with red and green
    bell peppers
3/4 cup water
1 teaspoon beef bouillon granules
Salt and pepper to taste
1 tablespoon chopped fresh parsley (optional)

Brown the ground beef in a large nonstick skillet over medium-high heat, stirring until crumbly; drain. Add the potatoes, corn, water and bouillon granules and mix well. Reduce the heat to medium. Cook, covered, for 20 minutes or until the potatoes are tender, stirring occasionally. Season with salt and pepper and sprinkle with the parsley.

*Kathy Orwig*

# SKILLET ENCHILADAS

1 pound ground beef
1/2 cup chopped onions
1 (10-ounce) can cream of mushroom soup
1 (10-ounce) can enchilada sauce
1/3 cup milk
8 to 10 corn tortillas
1/2 cup vegetable oil
2 1/2 to 3 1/2 cups (10 to 14 ounces) shredded
   Cheddar cheese

Brown the ground beef with the onions in a large skillet, stirring until the ground beef is crumbly; drain. Stir in the soup, enchilada sauce and milk. Bring to a boil and then reduce the heat. Cover and simmer for 20 minutes, stirring occasionally.

Warm the tortillas one at a time in a small amount of the oil in a skillet over medium heat, adding oil as needed. Remove each tortilla to a plate and place 1/4 cup of the cheese in the center. Roll the tortillas to enclose the cheese and place in the ground beef mixture in the skillet. Sprinkle the remaining cheese over the enchiladas. Cover and cook over low heat until the cheese is melted.

*Marla Storm*

# MEXICAN CASSEROLE

1 pound ground beef
1 onion, chopped
1 (10-ounce) can cream of mushroom soup
1 (10-ounce) can cream of tomato soup
1 (4-ounce) can chopped green chiles
12 corn tortillas
2 cups (8 ounces) shredded Cheddar cheese

Brown the ground beef with the onion, stirring until the ground beef is crumbly; drain. Stir in the mushroom soup, tomato soup and green chiles. Layer the tortillas and ground beef mixture one-half at a time in a greased baking dish. Sprinkle with the cheese. Bake at 350 degrees for 30 minutes.

*Linda Hardin*

# STORM FAMILY SPAGHETTI AND MEATBALLS

1 pound ground beef
1 slice bread, cut into small
  pieces
1 egg, beaten
1/4 cup water
2 tablespoons chili seasoning
Salt to taste
Vegetable oil

3 (15-ounce) cans tomato
  sauce
3 tablespoons chili seasoning
2 tablespoons sugar
2 tablespoons all-purpose flour
1/4 cup water
Hot cooked spaghetti

Combine the ground beef, bread, egg, 1/4 cup water, 2 tablespoons
chili seasoning and salt in a bowl and mix well. Shape into 1-inch
balls. Brown on all sides in hot oil in a skillet; drain. Combine the
tomato sauce, 3 tablespoons chili seasoning, the sugar and salt
in a skillet and bring to a boil; reduce the heat. Mix the flour and
1/4 cup water in a small bowl to a paste consistency. Add to the
tomato sauce mixture and cook over low heat until the sauce is
thickened, stirring constantly. Stir in the meatballs and simmer
for 30 minutes. Spoon over spaghetti in a serving bowl.

*Marla Storm*

# Baked Mostaccioli

2 pounds ground beef
1/2 cup chopped onion
1/4 cup chopped green
  bell pepper
1 garlic clove, minced
1 (28-ounce) can diced
  tomatoes
1 (8-ounce) can tomato sauce
1 (6-ounce) can tomato paste
1 (4-ounce) can mushrooms
1/2 cup water

1 teaspoon salt
1 teaspoon sugar
1 teaspoon basil
1/8 teaspoon pepper
1 bay leaf
8 ounces mostaccioli, cooked
  and drained
6 ounces mozzarella
  cheese, shredded
1/2 cup (2 ounces) grated
  Parmesan cheese

Brown the ground beef with the onion, bell pepper and garlic in a skillet, stirring until the ground beef is crumbly; drain. Stir in the tomatoes, tomato sauce, tomato paste, undrained mushrooms, water, salt, sugar, basil and pepper. Add the bay leaf. Bring to a boil and reduce the heat. Cover and simmer for 30 minutes, stirring occasionally. Remove from the heat; remove and discard the bay leaf. Stir in the mostaccioli. Layer one-half of the pasta mixture and one-half of the mozzarella cheese in a greased 3-quart baking dish. Top with the remaining pasta mixture. Sprinkle with the Parmesan cheese and cover with foil. Bake at 350 degrees for 30 minutes. Remove the foil and sprinkle the remaining mozzarella cheese over the top. Bake for 5 minutes. Let stand for 5 minutes before serving.

*Kathy Orwig*

# SKILLET LASAGNA

1 small onion, chopped
2 garlic cloves, minced
Dash of olive oil
1 pound Italian sausage, casings removed
Mushrooms, sliced
1 (26-ounce) jar tomato and basil marinara sauce
1 (8-ounce) can petite diced tomatoes
Italian seasoning (or basil and oregano) to taste
16 ounces bow tie pasta, ziti or rotini
2 cups (8 ounces) shredded mozzarella cheese

Sauté the onion and garlic in the olive oil in a skillet over medium heat until tender. Chop the sausage and stir it into the onion mixture. Brown the sausage on all sides; drain. Add mushrooms, the marinara sauce, tomatoes and Italian seasoning and mix well. Cook the pasta using the package directions; drain and return to the saucepan. Stir in the meat sauce. Top with the mozzarella. Cook, covered, over low heat until the cheese is bubbly. Spoon onto serving plates.

For a richer meat sauce, you may add $1/2$ cup ricotta cheese. You may substitute 1 pound ground beef or ground turkey for the Italian sausage.

*Joni Shaw*

# CRAZY CRUST PIZZA

1 pound ground round
1/4 cup chopped onion
1/4 cup chopped green bell pepper
1/2 teaspoon salt
1/2 teaspoon pepper
1/2 teaspoon oregano
1 cup all-purpose flour
2 egg whites
2/3 cup low-fat milk
1 (14-ounce) jar pizza sauce
Shredded cheese

Brown the beef with the onion and bell pepper in a skillet, stirring until the beef is crumbly; drain. Season with the salt, pepper and oregano. Combine the flour, egg whites and milk in a mixing bowl and beat at low speed until blended. Pour the batter into a baking dish coated with nonstick cooking spray and dusted with corn meal. Layer the beef mixture and pizza sauce over the batter. Sprinkle with cheese and other toppings as desired. Bake at 350 degrees for 30 minutes.

*Brian Shelton*

# MARINATED LAMB IN A SLOW COOKER

1 cup plain low-fat yogurt, at
  room temperature
1 teaspoon cornstarch
1 1/2 cups minced onions
1 cup chopped tomatoes
1 1/2 tablespoons minced
  fresh ginger
1 tablespoon vegetable oil

1 1/2 teaspoons cumin
3/4 teaspoon cayenne pepper
3/4 teaspoon turmeric
Salt to taste
2 pounds boneless lamb,
  cut into 2-inch cubes
1/3 cup chopped cilantro
1 teaspoon garam masala

Mix the yogurt and cornstarch in a small bowl. Combine the yogurt mixture, onions, tomatoes, ginger, oil, cumin, cayenne pepper, turmeric and salt in a large saucepan and mix well. Stir in the lamb. Let stand for 30 minutes to marinate. Cover and bring to a boil. Remove from the heat and spoon into a slow cooker. Cook on Low for 5 to 7 hours or until the lamb is fork-tender. Remove the lamb and place in a serving dish. Increase the heat and cook the remaining liquid until thickened. Spoon into a serving bowl and stir in the garam masala; spoon over the lamb. Garnish with the cilantro.

Instead of the garam masala, you can use 1/4 teaspoon cinnamon, 1/4 teaspoon ground cloves and 1/4 teaspoon black pepper. You may substitute 2 pounds beef for the lamb.

*Janet Warren*

# Pork Tenderloin Kabobs

1 (2-pound) pork tenderloin, trimmed and
    cut into 3/4- to 1-inch cubes
1 1/2 cups soy sauce
1 1/2 to 2 cups raw sugar
Juice of 1 or 2 lemons
1 1/2 tablespoons pepper
1 tablespoon minced garlic
6 to 8 shakes Tabasco sauce

Thread the pork onto 6- to 8-inch skewers. Place in a baking dish.
Mix the soy sauce, sugar, lemon juice, pepper, garlic and Tabasco
sauce in a small bowl. Pour over the pork and turn to coat. Marinate,
covered, in the refrigerator for 12 to 24 hours. Drain the pork,
discarding the marinade. Arrange the pork on a grill rack over hot
coals. Grill to the desired degree of doneness. Avoid burning the
meat due to the sugar in the marinade.

*Kerri Coffin*

# EASY MARINATED PORK TENDERLOIN

1 tablespoon minced garlic
2 1/4 teaspoons dried oregano
1 1/2 teaspoon salt
1 teaspoon black pepper
3/4 teaspoon dried rosemary
3/4 teaspoon dried thyme
1/4 teaspoon cayenne pepper
Drizzle of olive oil
1 (2-pound) pork tenderloin, trimmed

Combine the garlic, oregano, salt, black pepper, rosemary, thyme, cayenne pepper and olive oil in a small bowl and mix well. Rub over the pork, coating evenly. Place in a shallow dish. Marinate, covered, in the refrigerator for 30 minutes. Place the pork on a grill rack over hot coals. Grill for 10 minutes on each side or until cooked through. Serve hot or cold.

Any leftovers make great sandwiches.

*Janet Warren*

# SKILLET BARBECUED PORK CHOPS

4 to 6 (4-ounce) pork chops
1 tablespoon vegetable oil
1/3 cup chopped celery
2 tablespoons brown sugar
2 tablespoons lemon juice
1/2 teaspoon dry mustard
1/2 teaspoon salt
1/8 teaspoon pepper
2 (8-ounce) cans tomato sauce

Brown the pork chops in the oil in a large skillet over medium heat for 5 minutes on each side; drain. Sprinkle the celery, brown sugar, lemon juice, mustard, salt and pepper evenly over the pork chops. Pour the tomato sauce over the top. Simmer, covered, for 1 hour or until the pork chops are tender and cooked through.

*Kerri Coffin*

# Slow Cooker Ribs

2 pounds pork ribs
1 (10-ounce) can beef broth
1/2 cup water
3 tablespoons soy sauce

2 tablespoons maple syrup
2 tablespoons honey
2 tablespoons barbecue sauce

Place the ribs on a rack in a broiler pan. Broil for 15 minutes.
Combine the broth, water, soy sauce, syrup, honey and barbecue
sauce in a bowl and mix well. Pour over the ribs in a slow cooker.
Cook on Low for 8 to 10 hours or on High for 4 to 5 hours,
or until the ribs are tender and cooked through.

*Marla Storm*

# Barbecue Rub

1 tablespoon sea salt or
  kosher salt
1 tablespoon freshly ground
  black pepper
1 tablespoon garlic powder

1 tablespoon onion powder
1 tablespoon paprika
2 teaspoons chili powder
1 teaspoon cumin
1/4 teaspoon cayenne pepper

Mix the salt, black pepper, garlic powder, onion powder, paprika,
chili powder, cumin and cayenne pepper in a small bowl using your
fingers. This rub is good on any kind of meat and is excellent
for grilling.

*Chris Sale*

# Ham Tetrazzini

1 center-cut ham slice, cut into 1-inch squares
1 small onion, chopped
1/4 cup (1/2 stick) butter or margarine, melted
1 (10-ounce) can cream of mushroom soup (not fat-free)
1/2 soup can water
2 cups (8 ounces) shredded sharp Cheddar cheese
   (not fat-free)
Hot cooked spaghetti

Sauté the ham and onion in the butter in a large saucepan over medium heat until the edges of the ham crinkle. Stir in the soup, water, and cheese. Cook over low heat until thickened, stirring constantly. Spoon over spaghetti in a serving bowl.

This recipe may easily be doubled and is even better reheated.

*Kate and Flo Stanton*

# BACON REFRIED BEAN BURRITOS

6 slices bacon, cut into 1-inch pieces
2 (16-ounce) cans refried beans
Chopped onion
Shredded sharp Cheddar cheese
Flour tortillas
Salt and pepper to taste

Sauté the bacon in a skillet for 2 minutes or just until the bacon begins to crisp. Stir in the beans. Cook over medium heat for about 10 minutes, stirring frequently. Wrap tortillas in a damp paper towel and place on a microwave-safe plate. Microwave on High until warm. Spoon the bean mixture onto the tortillas on serving plates and top with onion and cheese. Season with salt and pepper. Other toppings such as sour cream, chopped jalapeño chiles and chopped tomatoes may be added as desired.

*Delores Clay*

# SNAPPY LEMON CHICKEN

3 to 5 pounds skinless chicken breasts and thighs
1/2 cup low-sodium soy sauce
1/4 cup lemon juice
2 tablespoons white wine
1 teaspoon Tabasco sauce
3 green onions, chopped
1 garlic clove, crushed

Rinse the chicken and pat dry. Combine the soy sauce, lemon juice, wine, Tabasco sauce, green onions and garlic in a sealable plastic bag. Add the chicken, turning to coat. Marinate in the refrigerator for 8 to 12 hours. Drain, reserving the marinade. Place the chicken on a grill rack. Grill over medium-hot coals until cooked through, turning once and basting with the marinade on both sides.

*Deana Trones*

# CHICKEN PARMESAN

1/3 cup bread crumbs
1/2 cup (2 ounces) grated
   Parmesan cheese
6 boneless skinless
   chicken breasts
1 egg, beaten
2 tablespoons olive oil
3/4 cup chopped onion

1 tablespoon olive oil
2 (15-ounce) cans
   tomato sauce
1 teaspoon oregano
1/4 teaspoon salt
1/4 teaspoon pepper
4 ounces mozzarella cheese,
   thinly sliced

Combine the bread crumbs and Parmesan cheese in a shallow
bowl. Dip the chicken into the egg and then dredge in the bread
crumb mixture. Cook the chicken in 2 tablespoons olive oil in
a skillet over medium-high heat for 5 to 7 minutes or until brown
on both sides. Place in a 9×13-inch baking pan.

Sauté the onion in 1 tablespoon olive oil in the skillet. Stir in the
tomato sauce, oregano, salt and pepper. Bring to a boil. Remove
from the heat. Pour three-quarters of the sauce over the chicken.
Arrange the mozzarella cheese slices over the sauce and pour the
remaining sauce over the cheese. Bake at 350 degrees for 20 minutes
or until the chicken is cooked through and the cheese is melted.

*Jessica Murray*

# PESTO CHICKEN WITH BASIL CREAM

PESTO CHICKEN
8 boneless skinless
  chicken breasts
8 (1-ounce) slices prosciutto
  or other ham
1 cup pesto
1/4 cup olive oil
2 garlic cloves, minced
1/4 teaspoon pepper

BASIL CREAM
1/3 cup dry white wine
2 shallots, finely chopped
1 1/2 cups whipping cream
1 cup finely chopped tomato
1/4 cup shredded fresh basil
1/4 teaspoon salt

To prepare the pesto chicken, pound the chicken between sheets of plastic wrap with a meat mallet or rolling pin to 1/4-inch thickness. Layer one slice prosciutto and 2 tablespoons of the pesto in the center of each piece of chicken. Roll the chicken crosswise to enclose the prosciutto and pesto and secure with a wooden pick. Mix the olive oil, garlic and pepper in a small bowl. Place the chicken on a grill rack or in a 9×13-inch baking pan. Grill over medium-hot coals, or bake at 350 degrees, for 15 to 20 minutes or until cooked through, turning and basting occasionally with the garlic mixture.

To prepare the basil cream, combine the wine and shallots in a saucepan and bring to a boil. Cook for 2 minutes or until the liquid is reduced to about 1/4 cup, stirring constantly. Add the cream and return to a boil. Reduce the heat and simmer for 8 to 10 minutes or until the liquid is reduced to about 1 cup, stirring constantly. Stir in the tomato, basil and salt. Cook just until heated through. Spoon over the chicken in a serving dish.

*Jennifer Dixon*

# JAPANESE CHICKEN

3 whole chicken breasts
1 egg, beaten
1/2 cup water
1/2 cup flour
1 teaspoon MSG
1/2 teaspoon salt
Corn oil for frying

Cut the chicken into bite-size pieces, discarding the skin and bones. Blend the egg, water, flour, MSG and salt in a shallow bowl. Dip the chicken into the batter. Fry in corn oil in a skillet over medium-high heat until golden brown on all sides and cooked through. Serve with soy sauce.

*Leslye Floyd*

# Swiss Chicken

1 (3-pound) chicken, cut up
Shortening
1 onion, chopped
1 (10-ounce) can tomato soup
1 cup water
1/4 cup sweet pickle relish
1 tablespoon brown sugar
1 tablespoon vinegar
1 tablespoon Worcestershire sauce

Cook the chicken in a small amount of shortening in a skillet over medium-high heat for 5 to 7 minutes or until light brown on all sides. Add the onion and sauté in the pan juices. Stir in the soup, water, pickle relish, brown sugar, vinegar and Worcestershire sauce. Cook, covered, over medium heat for 45 minutes or until the chicken is cooked through.

*Kerri Coffin*

# Jambalaya

1 large onion, chopped
1 cup chopped green bell pepper
2 garlic cloves, chopped
2 tablespoons vegetable oil
1 cup chopped cooked chicken
1 cup chopped cooked ham
1 cup sliced smoked sausage
2 1/2 cups chopped peeled tomatoes
2 1/2 cups chicken broth
1 cup rice
1 tablespoon chopped parsley
1 teaspoon salt
1/2 teaspoon Tabasco sauce

Sauté the onion, bell pepper and garlic in the oil in a large saucepan over medium heat until tender. Stir in the chicken, ham and sausage. Sauté for 5 minutes. Stir in the tomatoes, broth, rice, parsley, salt and Tabasco sauce. Bring to a boil and then reduce the heat. Cook, covered, for 20 to 25 minutes or until the rice is tender, stirring frequently.

*Marty Gustely*

# CHICKEN WITH YELLOW RICE AND BLACK BEANS

1 (3-pound) chicken, cooked
1 green bell pepper, chopped
1 red bell pepper, chopped
1 onion, chopped
1 tablespoon butter
4 cups water
1/4 cup vegetable oil

1 (8-ounce) package yellow rice
1 (13-ounce) can black beans
2 garlic cloves, minced
1 link sausage, cut into small
  pieces
Hot red pepper sauce to taste
Salt and pepper to taste

Chop the chicken, discarding the skin and bones. Sauté the bell peppers and onion in the butter in a skillet until soft. Bring the chicken and water to a boil in a large saucepan. Add the oil, rice and sautéed veetables. Cover the saucepan tightly and reduce the heat. Simmer for 25 minutes. Add the black beans, garlic, sausage, hot sauce, salt and pepper and stir gently to mix. Cover and cook over medium heat for 15 minutes, stirring occasionally.

*Deana Trones*

# CHICKEN ENCHILADAS

3 chicken breasts
4 ounces cheese, shredded
1 (4-ounce) can chopped green chiles
8 to 10 flour tortillas
1 (10-ounce) can cream of chicken soup
1 cup half-and-half or milk
4 ounces cheese, shredded

Boil the chicken in water to cover in a large saucepan for 20 to 25 minutes or until cooked through. Drain, reserving $1/2$ cup of the broth. Chop the chicken, discarding the skin and bones. Mix the chicken, 4 ounces cheese and the green chiles in a bowl. Arrange the tortillas on a work surface and spoon the chicken mixture down the center of each tortilla. Roll the tortillas to enclose the filling and arrange seam side down in a rectangular baking dish. Mix the soup, half-and-half and reserved broth in a small bowl. Pour over the enchiladas. Sprinkle with 4 ounces cheese. Bake at 350 degrees for 30 to 40 minutes or until heated through.

*Terry Suchala*

# Sour Cream Chicken Enchiladas

3 (5-ounce) cans chunk chicken, or
   1 pound boneless skinless chicken
   breasts, cooked and chopped
1/2 cup sour cream
2 (4-ounce) cans sliced mushrooms
1 (4-ounce) can chopped green chiles
1/3 cup chopped onion
2 garlic cloves, minced
1 teaspoon chili powder
1/2 teaspoon salt
1/4 teaspoon pepper
1 cup sour cream
12 corn tortillas
Vegetable oil
2 cups sour cream
1/3 pound Cheddar cheese, shredded

Combine the chicken, 1/2 cup sour cream, the mushrooms, green chiles, onion, garlic, chili powder, salt and pepper in a 2-quart saucepan and mix well. Cook over low heat until heated through, stirring occasionally. Spread 1 cup sour cream in a 9×13-inch baking dish. Heat the tortillas one at a time in 1 to 2 teaspoons of oil in a small skillet over medium-high heat, adding oil as needed. Arrange the tortillas on a work surface and spoon the chicken mixture down the center of each tortilla. Roll the tortillas to enclose the filling and arrange seam side down in the baking dish. Spread 2 cups sour cream over the enchiladas. Sprinkle with the cheese. Bake at 450 degrees for 8 minutes or until cheese is melted.

*Jessica Murray*

# Chicken Fajita Pasta with Chipotle Alfredo

1 large onion, thinly sliced
1 large green bell pepper, thinly sliced
1 large red bell pepper, thinly sliced
1 teaspoon olive oil
8 ounces marinated fajita chicken strips
3/4 cup fat-free evaporated milk
1 teaspoon chipotle sauce
1/8 teaspoon pepper
8 ounces rigatoni
1 yellow tomato, cut into 8 wedges (optional)
1/4 cup sliced black olives

Sauté the onion and bell peppers in the olive oil in a skillet over medium heat for 2 to 3 minutes or until tender. Push to one side of the skillet and add the chicken. Sauté for 6 to 8 minutes or until cooked through. Stir the onion mixture and chicken together and remove from the heat. Mix the evaporated milk, chipotle sauce and pepper in a small bowl. Cook the pasta using the package directions, omitting the salt and oil. Drain and return to the saucepan. Stir in the chicken mixture and the alfredo sauce. Cook over low heat for 1 to 2 minutes or until heated through. Spoon into a large serving bowl and top with the tomato and olives.

*Tracy Orwig*

# Lemon Chicken Stir-Fry

8 ounces bow tie pasta
1 pound boneless chicken
 breasts, cut into
 1-inch-wide strips
1 teaspoon vegetable oil
2 large carrots, peeled and
 sliced (about 1 cup)
2 small red bell peppers, cut
 into quarters and sliced
1 teaspoon vegetable oil

8 ounces asparagus, trimmed
 and cut into 1-inch lengths
1 small yellow squash, cut into
 halves lengthwise and sliced
1/2 cup water
1 envelope savory herb and
 garlic soup mix
2 teaspoons lemon juice
1/4 cup (1 ounce) freshly grated
 Parmesan cheese

Cook the pasta using the package directions. Drain and then spoon the pasta into a bowl; cover and keep warm. Stir-fry the chicken in 1 teaspoon oil in a large skillet or wok over medium-high heat until cooked through. Spoon over the pasta; cover and keep warm. Stir-fry the carrots and bell peppers in 1 teaspoon oil in the skillet for 2 to 3 minutes. Add the asparagus and squash and stir fry for 1 to 2 minutes or until tender-crisp. Whisk the water, soup mix and lemon juice in a small bowl. Add the soup mixture to the vegetables in the skillet and reduce the heat to low. Simmer, covered, for 5 minutes or until thickened, stirring frequently. Add the pasta and chicken and toss to coat. Sprinkle with the cheese. Serve immediately.

*Stella Carr*

# RANCH NOODLE CHICKEN

16 ounces bow tie pasta
4 boneless chicken breasts, cooked and chopped
1 (15-ounce) can peas
1 (14-ounce) can sliced carrots
2 envelopes ranch salad dressing mix

Cook the pasta using the package directions. Drain and then transfer to a large serving bowl. Stir the chicken, peas and carrots into the hot pasta. Sprinkle with the salad dressing mix and mix well.

*Staci Williams*

# CHICKEN NOODLE BAKE

6 to 8 chicken breasts
1 (8-ounce) package egg noodles
2 (10-ounce) cans cream of mushroom soup
8 ounces cream cheese, softened
1 cup sour cream
1/2 teaspoon garlic salt
1 small onion, chopped
Croutons or toasted buttered bread crumbs
Paprika to taste

Boil the chicken in water to cover in a large saucepan for about 1 hour or until cooked through. Drain, reserving the broth. Chop the chicken, discarding the skin and bones. Cook the noodles in the broth in the saucepan using the package directions; drain. Combine the soup, cream cheese, sour cream and garlic salt in a mixing bowl and beat until blended; stir in the onion. Fold in the noodles. Spoon one-half of the noodle mixture into a baking dish. Layer with the chicken and then the remaining noodle mixture. Top with croutons and sprinkle with paprika. Bake at 350 degrees for 45 minutes.

*Elizabeth Orwig*

# BUSY MOMS' CHICKEN TETRAZZINI

16 ounces spaghetti, cooked and drained
5 chicken breasts, cooked and chopped
2 (10-ounce) cans cream of chicken soup
2$^{1}$/4 cups water
$^{1}$/4 cup ($^{1}$/2 stick) butter
2 chicken bouillon cubes
$^{1}$/2 cup (2 ounces) shredded Cheddar cheese

Layer the spaghetti and chicken in a 9×13-inch baking pan.

Combine the soup, water, butter and bouillon cubes in a saucepan and mix well. Bring to a boil and cook until the butter is melted and the bouillon cubes are dissolved, stirring constantly. Pour over the chicken and spaghetti. Sprinkle with the cheese. Press lightly with a spatula or back of a spoon. Bake at 350 degrees for 25 to 30 minutes or until heated through.

*Deanna Barrow*

# CHICKEN AND DUMPLINGS WITH VEGETABLES

4 boneless skinless chicken
  breasts, cut into
  1-inch pieces
1 1/2 cups chopped onions
1 cup chopped celery
3 garlic cloves, minced
2 tablespoons margarine, melted
1 (16-ounce) package frozen
  mixed vegetables

6 cups chicken broth
3 tablespoons chopped fresh
  parsley, or 3 teaspoons
  parsley flakes
1 teaspoon poultry seasoning
1 cup skim milk
1/3 cup flour
1 (10-count) can refrigerator
  buttermilk biscuits

Sauté the chicken, onions, celery and garlic in the margarine in a large saucepan over medium heat for 7 to 12 minutes or until the chicken is cooked through. Stir in the mixed vegetables, broth, parsley and poultry seasoning. Bring to a boil, stirring frequently. Blend the milk and flour in a small bowl; stir into the chicken mixture. Cook over medium-high heat until the sauce boils and thickens, stirring constantly. Reduce the heat to low. Separate the biscuits; flatten and cut each in half crosswise. Arrange on top of the chicken mixture, starting in the center. Cover and cook for 20 to 25 minutes or until biscuits are light brown and fluffy.

*Kathy Orwig*

# CHICKEN AND JALAPEÑO CORN BREAD CASSEROLE

1 (3-pound) chicken
1 large onion, chopped
1 green bell pepper, chopped
Salt and pepper to taste
2 (6-ounce) packages yellow corn bread mix
1 (6-ounce) package white corn bread mix
2 cups seasoned bread crumbs
1 onion, chopped
6 boiled eggs, chopped
6 ribs celery, chopped
1 cup chopped pickled jalapeño chiles, or to taste

Boil the chicken, 1 onion, the bell pepper, salt and pepper in water to cover in a large saucepan until the chicken is cooked through and falling off the bone. Drain, reserving the broth. Strain the broth, discarding the solids. Chop the chicken, discarding the skin and bones. Prepare the corn bread using the package directions. Crumble into a large bowl. Stir in the chicken, bread crumbs, 1 onion, the eggs, celery and jalapeño chiles.

Stir in enough of the reserved broth to make the chicken mixture moist, but not soupy. Spoon into a baking dish. Bake at 375 degrees for 55 minutes.

*Sheilia Trevino*

# CHICKEN AND DRESSING CASSEROLE

4 or 5 large chicken breasts
2 (6-ounce) packages herb-seasoned stuffing mix
1 (10-ounce) can cream of mushroom soup
1 (10-ounce) can cream of celery soup

Boil the chicken in water in a large saucepan until the chicken is cooked through; drain. Cut the chicken into bite-size pieces, discarding the skin and bones. Prepare the stuffing using the package directions and spoon into a 9×13-inch baking dish. Mix the chicken, cream of mushroom soup and cream of celery soup in a bowl. Spread over the stuffing. Bake at 350 degrees for 30 to 40 minutes or until heated through.

*Linda Hardin*

# GRILLED ITALIAN CHICKEN SANDWICHES

1 pound boneless skinless chicken breasts
1 1/2 pounds eggplant and/or zucchini, cut into thick slices
1 cup Italian salad dressing
1 (12-ounce) jar roasted red peppers, drained and rinsed
8 ounces mozzarella cheese, sliced
Green leaf lettuce
8 slices peasant bread, grilled

Place the chicken and eggplant in a large glass dish. Add 3/4 cup of the salad dressing. Marinate, covered, in the refrigerator for 1 to 3 hours; drain. Place the chicken and eggplant on a rack on a broiler pan or on a grill rack. Broil or grill for 12 minutes or until the chicken is cooked through and the eggplant is tender, turning and basting with the remaining 1/4 cup salad dressing. Layer the chicken, eggplant, peppers, cheese and lettuce evenly on four slices of the bread. Top with the remaining four slices of bread.

*Kathy Chaffee*

# AMERICAN GOULASH

1 pound ground turkey breast
1/4 cup chopped red onion
1 teaspoon minced garlic, or to taste
1 teaspoon basil
1 teaspoon oregano
2 teaspoons olive oil
1 (15-ounce) can black beans, drained and rinsed
1 (15-ounce) can whole kernel corn, drained
1 (14-ounce) can stewed tomatoes
1 teaspoon Tabasco sauce
Pinch of salt
Dash of pepper

Brown the turkey with the onion, garlic, basil and oregano in the olive oil in a skillet over medium heat, stirring until the turkey is cooked through and crumbly. Stir in the beans, corn, undrained tomatoes, Tabasco sauce, salt and pepper. Bring to a boil and then reduce the heat. Simmer for about 7 minutes or until heated through, stirring frequently. Spoon into serving bowls.

*Shayla McDonald*

# SEAFOOD

# BLACKENED CATFISH

2 pounds catfish fillets
2 tablespoons butter, melted
4 teaspoons lemon thyme or thyme
2 teaspoons cayenne pepper
2 teaspoons garlic powder
2 teaspoons black pepper
1 teaspoon salt
1/2 cup Italian salad dressing

Brush both sides of the catfish with the butter. Mix the lemon thyme, cayenne pepper, garlic powder, black pepper and salt in a shallow bowl. Dip the fillets in the seasoning mixture to coat both sides. Cook in a skillet over medium heat for 2 minutes on each side or until slightly blackened. Arrange in a single layer in a lightly greased baking dish and cover with the salad dressing. Bake at 350 degrees for 30 to 40 minutes or until the catfish begins to flake.

*Janet Warren*

# GRILLED SALMON WITH EGGPLANT CAVIAR

1 onion, finely chopped
1/4 cup olive oil
1 (16-ounce) can diced tomatoes
1 eggplant, peeled and finely chopped
2 tablespoons lemon juice
1/2 teaspoon salt
Pepper to taste
3 salmon steaks, grilled

Sauté the onion in the olive oil in a large skillet over medium-high heat for 5 minutes. Add the tomatoes and sauté for 5 minutes. Lower the heat to medium and stir in the eggplant, lemon juice, salt and pepper. Cook, covered, for about 20 minutes, stirring occasionally. Purée one-half of the eggplant mixture in a blender or food processor. Return to the pan and mix well. Serve over the salmon steaks. The eggplant caviar can be frozen for later use.

*Janet Warren*

# Rosemary-Roasted Salmon

2 large bunches fresh rosemary
1 large red onion, thinly sliced
1 (2-pound) center-cut salmon fillet
Salt and pepper to taste
2 large lemons, thinly sliced
1/3 cup olive oil

Arrange one-half of the rosemary sprigs in a single layer in the center of a heavy baking sheet. Arrange the onion slices over the rosemary. Place the salmon skin side down on top of the onions. Sprinkle with salt and pepper and cover with the remaining rosemary sprigs. Arrange the lemon slices over the rosemary and sprinkle with salt. Drizzle with the olive oil. Roast the salmon at 500 degrees for about 20 minutes, or just until cooked through. Transfer the salmon to a serving platter. Discard the rosemary. Serve with the roasted onions and lemon slices.

*Janet Warren*

# SALMON WITH TOMATOES

1 cup rice
2 cups water
2 (6-ounce) skinless
   salmon fillets
1/2 teaspoon dried dill weed
1/4 teaspoon paprika, or
   to taste
Salt and pepper to taste
2 1/2 tablespoons garlic oil

2 tomatoes, chopped
1 1/2 teaspoons minced garlic
1 teaspoon lemon juice
1/4 cup (1 ounce) grated
   Parmesan cheese
3 tablespoons chopped
   fresh parsley
4 dashes hot red pepper sauce
2 tablespoons butter

Combine the rice and water in a saucepan and bring to a boil.
Reduce the heat to low. Cook, covered, for 20 minutes or until
the water is absorbed. Spoon into a serving bowl and keep warm.

Season the salmon with the dill weed, paprika, salt and pepper.
Cook in the garlic oil in a skillet over medium heat for 1 to
2 minutes on each side or just until tender. Break the salmon into
bite-size pieces with a spatula or fork. Stir in the tomatoes, garlic
and lemon juice. Cook until the salmon begins to flake. Stir in
the cheese, parsley and hot sauce. Add the butter. Cook for 1 to
2 minutes or until the butter is melted, stirring constantly. Spoon
over the rice to serve.

*Megan Sullivan*

# SOLE FLORENTINE

1 cup chopped red bell pepper
2 garlic cloves, minced
1 tablespoon olive oil
4 cups loosely packed fresh
   spinach, trimmed
1/2 teaspoon dried thyme
1/3 teaspoon salt
1/4 cup whole wheat
   bread crumbs

1 egg white
2 tablespoons grated
   Parmesan cheese
4 (4-ounce) sole fillets
2 tablespoons dry white wine
1 tablespoon fat-free chicken
   broth or vegetable broth

Sauté the bell pepper and garlic in the olive oil in a nonstick skillet over medium heat for 2 to 3 minutes or until tender. Spoon 1/4 cup of the bell pepper mixture into a small bowl and reserve. Stir the spinach, thyme and salt into the remaining bell pepper mixture in the skillet and cook for 1 minute or until the spinach is wilted. Spoon into a bowl. Stir in the bread crumbs, egg white and cheese.

Cut the fillets in half lengthwise. Spoon 2 tablespoons of the spinach mixture onto the wide end of the fillet and roll to enclose the filling. Place the rolls seam side down in a 7×11-inch baking dish coated with nonstick cooking spray. Sprinkle with the reserved bell pepper mixture and drizzle with the wine and broth. Cover with foil. Bake at 425 degrees for 10 to 12 minutes or just until the fish begins to flake.

*Janet Warren*

# Parmesan-Crusted Tilapia with Lemon Caper Sauce

**Parmesan-Crusted Tilapia**
1 1/2 cups (6 ounces) grated
  Parmesan cheese
1/2 cup all-purpose flour
2 (5- to 6-ounce) tilapia fillets
All-purpose flour for dredging
1 egg, lightly beaten
1 tablespoon olive oil

**Lemon Caper Sauce**
Olive oil
1 teaspoon minced garlic
1/4 cup chicken stock
2 tablespoons white wine
1 1/2 teaspoon capers, drained
Juice of 1/2 a lemon
Pinch of salt
Pinch of pepper
1 tablespoon unsalted butter

To prepare the tilapia, mix the cheese and 1/2 cup flour in a shallow bowl. Dredge the fillets in additional flour in a shallow bowl and then dip into the egg. Coat with the cheese mixture. Fry the fillets on both sides in the olive oil in a nonstick skillet over high heat until golden brown. Remove to a serving platter and keep warm.

To prepare the sauce, sauté the garlic in the same skillet over medium heat, adding olive oil if needed. Add the chicken stock, wine, capers, lemon juice, salt and pepper. Cook until the liquid is reduced by one-half. Remove from the heat. Add the butter and stir until melted. Spoon over the fillets. Serve with orzo and asparagus.

*Tracy Orwig*

# CRAB CAKES WITH CUCUMBER SAUCE

CRAB CAKES
4 slices dry white bread,
  crusts trimmed
1/2 teaspoon dry mustard
1/2 teaspoon Old Bay Seasoning
1/2 cup mayonnaise
1 egg, beaten
1/2 teaspoon
  Worcestershire sauce
1/2 teaspoon lemon juice
1/4 cup minced red bell pepper
1 shallot, minced
1 pound crab meat, drained
  and flaked

2 tablespoons butter
2 tablespoons vegetable oil

CUCUMBER SAUCE
1/2 cup rice vinegar
5 tablespoons sugar
2 tablespoons fresh lime juice
2 tablespoons water
1/4 cup grated seeded
  peeled cucumber
2 teaspoons minced jalapeño
  chiles (optional)
1 teaspoon minced garlic
1 teaspoon sesame seeds

To prepare the crab cakes, process the bread in a food processor to make fine crumbs. Remove to a small bowl and stir in the mustard and Old Bay seasoning. Mix the mayonnaise, egg, Worcestershire sauce and lemon juice in a large bowl. Stir in the bread crumb mixture, bell pepper, shallot and crab meat. Shape into ten cakes. Place on a baking sheet covered with baking parchment and wrap with plastic wrap. Chill for 2 hours. Fry in two batches in the butter and oil in a heavy skillet over medium heat for 4 minutes on each side or until golden brown. Drain on a plate covered with paper towels. Keep warm in a 250-degree oven until ready to serve.

To prepare the cucumber sauce, combine the vinegar, sugar, lime juice and water in a small bowl and stir until the sugar dissolves. Stir in the cucumber, jalapeño chiles, garlic and sesame seeds. Let stand at room temperature for 30 minutes. Serve with the crab cakes.

*Dawn Chaffee*

# CRAB AND SHRIMP DELIGHT

1 (10-ounce) can cream of shrimp soup
1 cup milk
1 cup mayonnaise
8 ounces fresh crab meat, drained and flaked
8 ounces cooked salad shrimp
8 ounces angel hair pasta, broken into small pieces
2 cups (8 ounces) shredded sharp Cheddar cheese
1 (6-ounce) can French-fried onions

Blend the soup, milk and mayonnaise in a large bowl. Stir in the crab meat, shrimp and pasta. Spoon into a 9×12-inch baking dish. Sprinkle with the cheese. Bake, covered, at 350 degrees for 35 minutes. Uncover and sprinkle with the onions. Bake for 10 more minutes.

*Megan Sullivan*

# SHRIMP AND CRAB MEAT LOAF

1 (6-ounce) can small shrimp, drained
1 (6-ounce) can crab meat, drained and flaked
1/2 cup mayonnaise
1/4 cup thinly sliced green onions
1/4 cup chopped celery
8 ounces mozzarella cheese, shredded
1/8 teaspoon salt
1/8 teaspoon freshly ground pepper
1 (1-pound) loaf French bread, cut into halves horizontally

Combine the shrimp, crab meat, mayonnaise, green onions, celery, cheese, salt and pepper in a bowl and mix well. Spread on the bottom half of the bread and cover with the top half. Cut the loaf into eight pieces and serve immediately. The loaf can also be refrigerated before serving. To heat, wrap in aluminum foil and bake for 20 minutes at 400 degrees or until heated through. Cut into eight pieces and serve.

*Megan Sullivan*

# SHRIMP AND CRAB ENCHILADAS

12 (12-inch) flour tortillas
8 ounces Monterey Jack cheese, shredded
1 (6-ounce) can crab meat, drained and flaked
1 pound cooked shrimp, peeled and deveined
1 (20-ounce) can green enchilada sauce
1 cup sour cream
1 bunch green onions, chopped

Arrange the tortillas on a work surface. Place equal amounts of the cheese, crab meat and shrimp in the center of each tortilla, reserving some cheese for the top. Roll the tortillas to enclose the filling and arrange seam side down in a 9×13-inch baking pan. Pour the enchilada sauce over the enchiladas; the sauce should completely cover the enchiladas. Sprinkle with the reserved cheese. Bake, covered, at 350 degrees for 30 minutes. Uncover and bake for 15 more minutes. Top with sour cream and green onions to serve.

*Megan Sullivan*

# SHRIMP JAMBALAYA

8 ounces smoked sausage, turkey sausage or andouille
2 tablespoons vegetable oil
1 cup chopped green bell pepper
1/2 cup chopped green onions
2 garlic cloves, minced
1 1/2 cups canned diced tomatoes
1/4 cup chopped fresh parsley
1 teaspoon thyme
1/2 teaspoon salt
1/8 teaspoon cayenne pepper
1 bay leaf
1 1/2 cups water
1 cup rice
2 pounds shrimp, peeled and deveined

Chop the sausage. Sauté in the oil in a large saucepan over medium heat for about 3 minutes. Add the bell pepper, green onions and garlic and sauté until tender. Stir in the tomatoes, parsley, thyme, salt, cayenne pepper and bay leaf. Add the water and rice and mix well. Stir in the shrimp and bring to a boil. Reduce the heat to low and cover tightly. Cook without stirring for 25 to 30 minutes or until the rice is fluffy.

*Chris Sale*

# SHRIMP KABOBS

1/4 cup plum preserves
1 tablespoon minced garlic
1 tablespoon Jack Daniel's Dijon mustard
1 teaspoon soy sauce
3 shakes of seasoning salt
12 jumbo shrimp, deveined
Cherry tomatoes
Mushrooms, trimmed
Pineapple chunks
Zucchini, cut into thick slices

Whisk the plum preserves, garlic, Dijon mustard, soy sauce and seasoning salt in a bowl. Reserve 1/2 cup of the marinade for basting the kabobs. Stir the shrimp into the remaining marinade. Marinate, covered, in the refrigerator for 45 minutes. Drain the shrimp, discarding the marinade. Thread the shrimp, tomatoes, mushrooms, pineapple and zucchini alternately onto two skewers. Place on a grill rack. Grill over hot coals until the shrimp turn pink, turning and basting with the reserved marinade.

*Kerry Roberson*

# SHRIMP SCAMPI

1 pound shrimp, peeled and deveined
1 onion, chopped
1/2 teaspoon garlic salt, or minced garlic to taste
2 tablespoons butter or margarine, melted
1 envelope chicken gravy mix
1 1/2 cups water
1 red or green bell pepper, chopped
1 tablespoon lemon juice
Salt to taste
1 1/2 cups quick-cooking rice
1/4 cup chopped parsley

Sauté the shrimp, onion and garlic in the butter in a large skillet over medium heat until the shrimp turn pink. Combine the gravy mix and water in a small bowl and mix well. Add to the shrimp mixture. Stir in the bell pepper, lemon juice and salt and bring to a boil. Stir in the rice and parsley. Cover and remove from the heat. Let stand for 5 minutes and then fluff with a fork.

*Roger Harmon*

# ANGEL HAIR PASTA WITH SHRIMP AND BASIL

8 ounces angel hair pasta
1 tablespoon olive oil
1 teaspoon chopped garlic
3 tablespoons olive oil
1 pound large shrimp, peeled and deveined
2 (28-ounce) cans Italian-style diced tomatoes, drained
1/2 cup dry white wine
1/4 cup chopped parsley
3 tablespoons chopped fresh basil
3 tablespoons freshly grated Parmesan cheese

Cook the pasta in a large saucepan of boiling water with 1 tablespoon olive oil. Drain and rinse briefly with cold water. Transfer to a serving bowl. Sauté the garlic in 3 tablespoons olive oil in a skillet over medium heat for about 1 minute or until tender. Add the shrimp and sauté for 3 to 5 minutes. Remove the shrimp to a bowl and keep warm. Add the tomatoes, wine, parsley and basil to the skillet. Cook for 8 to 12 minutes or until the liquid is reduced by one-half, stirring occasionally. Add the shrimp and cook for 2 to 3 minutes or until the shrimp are heated through, stirring occasionally. Spoon over the pasta. Sprinkle with the cheese.

*Megan Sullivan*

# Pasta with Grilled Shrimp and Pineapple Salsa

3 cups rotini
Salt to taste
1/2 fresh pineapple, cored and chopped
1 large red bell pepper, chopped
1 large red onion, chopped
1 jalapeño chile, seeded and minced
1/2 cup fresh orange juice
1/3 cup fresh lime juice
1 1/2 pounds large shrimp, peeled and deveined

Cook the pasta in a large saucepan of lightly salted water for 8 to 10 minutes or until al dente; drain. Combine the pineapple, bell pepper, onion and jalapeño chile in a large bowl. Stir in the orange juice and lime juice. Toss the pasta with the pineapple salsa. Place the shrimp on an oiled grill rack. Grill 6 inches from the hot coals for 2 minutes on each side. Top the pasta with the shrimp.

*Megan Sullivan*

# Spicy Stuffed Shrimp with Raspberry Chipotle Sauce

3 pounds jumbo shrimp, peeled, deveined and chilled
1 pound jalapeño chiles, seeded
16 ounces habanero Jack cheese or other spicy hot cheese,
   thinly sliced
2 pounds thickly sliced bacon
1 (12-ounce) bottle roasted raspberry chipotle sauce

Soak wooden skewers in water for about 2 hours. Cut the shrimp along the back with a sharp knife until almost butterflied. Cut the jalapeño chiles into very thin strips, about the width of a wooden pick. Cut the cheese into strips about twice the width of the jalapeño chile strips. Stuff a cheese strip and a jalapeño chile strip into the cut in the shrimp. Cut the bacon slices into halves crosswise and wrap each shrimp with half a slice. Thread six wrapped shrimp onto each skewer. Place on a grill rack. Grill over hot coals until the shrimp turn pink and the bacon is cooked through, turning once. Place on a serving platter and drizzle with the chipotle sauce.

*Chris Kraft*

# SWEET-AND-SPICY SHRIMP

1/4 cup soy sauce
2 teaspoons sugar
2 teaspoons cornstarch
1/2 teaspoon sesame oil
1/2 teaspoon crushed red pepper
1 small onion, cut into 1-inch pieces
1/2 green bell pepper, cut into 1-inch pieces
1 carrot, thinly sliced (about 1/2 cup)
1 tablespoon vegetable oil
12 to 16 ounces large shrimp, peeled and deveined
1 egg, scrambled (optional)
1/2 cup frozen green peas, thawed (optional)
Hot cooked rice

Whisk the soy sauce, sugar, cornstarch, sesame oil and red pepper
in a small bowl until the cornstarch is dissolved. Sauté the onion, bell
pepper and carrot in the vegetable oil in a large skillet over medium-
high heat for 2 to 3 minutes or until tender-crisp. Stir in the soy sauce
mixture, shrimp, egg and peas. Stir-fry for 3 to 5 minutes or until
the shrimp turn pink and the sauce is thickened. Serve over rice.

*Roger Harmon*

# SPICY TEQUILA SHRIMP

1 1/2 pounds deveined peeled large shrimp
1/4 cup apple cider vinegar
2 tablespoons tequila
2 tablespoons liquid from a jar of pickled jalapeño chiles
2 tablespoons olive oil
2 tablespoons honey mustard
2 teaspoons cayenne pepper
1 teaspoon sea salt or kosher salt
1 teaspoon freshly ground black pepper
1 teaspoon garlic powder
1 teaspoon onion powder
8 splashes of Tabasco sauce

Thread the shrimp onto skewers and place in a deep glass dish. Whisk the vinegar, tequila, jalapeño chile liquid, olive oil, mustard, cayenne pepper, salt, black pepper, garlic powder, onion powder and Tabasco sauce in a bowl. Pour over the shrimp, covering completely. Marinate, covered, in the refrigerator for 15 minutes. Drain the shrimp and place on a grill rack, discarding the marinade. Grill over hot coals for 3 minutes on each side, or until the shrimp turn pink. Remove to a serving platter. Let stand for 2 minutes before serving.

*Chris Sale*

# SHRIMP AND SCALLOP KABOBS

1 pound large shrimp, peeled and deveined
8 ounces scallops
1 red bell pepper, cut into 1-inch pieces
1 green bell pepper, cut into 1-inch pieces
1 fresh pineapple, cored and cut into wedges
1/2 cup rice vinegar
3 tablespoons light soy sauce
2 teaspoons sesame oil
2 teaspoons minced fresh ginger

Soak six wooden skewers in warm water for 15 minutes, or use metal skewers. Thread the shrimp, scallops, bell peppers and pineapple alternately onto the skewers. Whisk the vinegar, soy sauce, sesame oil and ginger in a small bowl. Place the kabobs on an oiled grill rack and baste with some of the sauce. Grill 4 inches from the heat source for 5 to 6 minutes, turning and basting with more of the sauce while grilling. Heat the remaining sauce in a small saucepan over low heat. Serve with the kabobs.

*Megan Sullivan*

# DESSERTS

# VERY BERRY ANGEL FOOD CAKE

1 cup cake flour
1/2 cup raw sugar
1 tablespoon cornstarch
3/4 teaspoon salt
12 egg whites, at room
 temperature

1 teaspoon cream of tartar
3/4 cup raw sugar
1 1/2 teaspoons vanilla extract
1 cup chopped strawberries
 and/or whole raspberries

Combine 1 cup cake flour, 1/2 cup sugar, the cornstarch and salt in a large bowl. Beat the egg whites at low speed in a mixing bowl for 3 minutes or until foamy. Add the cream of tartar, 3/4 cup sugar and the vanilla. Beat at medium-high speed until stiff peaks form. Do not overbeat. Sift one-third of the dry ingredients over the egg white mixture and gently fold in. Sift one-half of the remaining dry ingredients over the batter and gently fold in. Spoon the strawberries evenly over the top of the batter. Sift the remaining dry ingredients over the strawberries. Fold into the batter.

Spoon the batter gently into an ungreased 10-inch tube pan and place on the middle rack of the oven. Bake at 350 degrees for 40 to 50 minutes or until the cake is golden brown and springs back when lightly touched. Invert onto a funnel and let stand for about 90 minutes or until cooled completely. Loosen the cake from the side of the pan and arrange on a cake plate. Serve with low-fat or nonfat whipped topping and additional fresh berries.

*Deana Trones*

# LOW-FAT CARROT CAKE

2 cups all-purpose flour
1 3/4 cups sugar
1 teaspoon baking powder
1 teaspoon baking soda
1 teaspoon cinnamon
3 cups shredded carrots
1/2 cup light vegetable oil
1/2 cup unsweetened applesauce
4 eggs, lightly beaten, or an equivalent
   amount of egg substitute

Combine the flour, sugar, baking powder, baking soda and cinnamon in a large mixing bowl. Add the carrots, oil, applesauce and eggs. Beat at low speed until combined. Increase the speed to medium and beat for 2 minutes. Spoon into a greased and lightly floured 9×13-inch cake pan. Bake at 325 degrees for 50 minutes or until the cake tests done. Cool in the pan for 10 minutes. Remove to a wire rack to cool completely.

*Brian Shelton*

# HEATH BAR CAKE

1 tablespoon (or more)
  baking cocoa
2 cups sifted all-purpose flour
1 1/4 teaspoons baking soda
1/4 teaspoon salt
1/2 cup (1 stick) unsalted
  butter, softened
1 cup packed light brown sugar
1/2 cup granulated sugar
1 teaspoon vanilla extract

2 eggs, at room temperature
1 1/2 cups buttermilk, at room
  temperature
1/2 cup chopped pecans
  or chopped walnuts
7 (1.4-ounce) Heath bars or
  other chocolate-covered
  toffee candy bars, chopped
  and chilled

Grease a 9×13-inch baking pan or coat with nonstick baking spray. Dust the pan with the cocoa, discarding any cocoa that does not adhere to the side of the pan. Mix the flour, baking soda and salt in a small bowl.

Cream the butter, brown sugar and granulated sugar in a mixing bowl at high speed for about 5 minutes or until light and fluffy. Reduce the speed to medium and add the vanilla. Beat in the eggs one at a time. Add the flour mixture and buttermilk alternately one-third at a time, mixing after each addition just until combined. Stop the mixer occasionally to scrape down the side of the bowl. Stir in the pecans and one-half of the Heath bar pieces. (The batter will be thick.)

Spoon into the prepared pan and smooth the top. Scatter the remaining Heath bar pieces over the top. Bake at 325 degrees for 40 to 45 minutes or until a wooden pick inserted in the center comes out clean. Cool in the pan for 45 minutes or more before cutting. Sprinkle the cake with additional cocoa if desired.

*Chris Kraft*

# OCEAN CAKE

## CAKE
2 cups sifted all-purpose flour
2 cups sugar
1/4 teaspoon salt
1 cup water
1/2 cup (1 stick) margarine
1/2 cup vegetable oil
1/4 cup baking cocoa
1/2 cup reduced-fat buttermilk
1 teaspoon baking soda
2 eggs, lightly beaten
1 teaspoon vanilla extract

## CHOCOLATE FROSTING
1/2 cup (1 stick) margarine
6 tablespoons skim milk
1/4 cup baking cocoa
1 (1-pound) package
   confectioners' sugar, sifted
1 teaspoon vanilla extract
1/8 teaspoon salt

To prepare the cake, sift the flour, sugar and salt together into a large mixing bowl. Combine the water, margarine, oil and baking cocoa in a saucepan and bring to a boil. Pour into the flour mixture immediately. Beat at medium speed until blended. Mix the buttermilk and baking soda in a small bowl and then add to the batter. Add the eggs and vanilla and beat until smooth. Spoon into a greased deep 9×13-inch or an 11×16-inch cake pan. Bake at 350 degrees for 20 to 35 minutes or until a wooden pick inserted in the center comes out clean.

To prepare the frosting, combine the margarine, milk and baking cocoa in a saucepan and bring to a boil, stirring constantly. Remove from the heat and pour into a mixing bowl. Add the confectioners' sugar, vanilla and salt gradually, beating constantly until smooth. Spread over the hot cake. Cut into squares to serve.

*Ginger Holley*

# ALMOND AMARETTO POUND CAKE

CAKE
1 (2-layer) package yellow cake mix
$1/2$ cup sugar
8 ounces cream cheese, softened
4 eggs, lightly beaten
$1/2$ cup water
$1/2$ cup oil
2 teaspoons almond extract
1 teaspoon vanilla extract

AMARETTO GLAZE
$1/2$ cup water
$1/2$ cup sugar
3 tablespoons amaretto

To prepare the cake, combine the cake mix and sugar in a mixing bowl. Add the cream cheese, eggs, water and oil and beat until smooth. Stir in the flavorings. Spoon into a greased and floured bundt pan. Bake at 350 degrees for 45 minutes or until the cake tests done. Cool in the pan for 5 minutes. Invert onto a serving plate.

To prepare the glaze, combine the water and sugar in a saucepan. Bring to a boil and cook until the sugar dissolves, stirring constantly. Stir in the amaretto. Drizzle over the warm cake.

*Margaret Dorland*

# AUNTIE'S COCONUT POUND CAKE

CAKE
3 cups all-purpose flour
1/2 teaspoon baking powder
1/2 teaspoon salt
1 cup (2 sticks) butter,
  softened
1/2 cup shortening
3 cups sugar
5 eggs

1/2 cup milk
1 teaspoon coconut extract
1 teaspoon rum extract

ALMOND GLAZE
1 cup water
1 cup sugar
1 teaspoon almond extract

To prepare the cake, mix the flour, baking powder and salt together into a bowl. Cream the butter, shortening and sugar in a mixing bowl until light and fluffy. Add the eggs one at a time, mixing well after each addition. Add the flour mixture alternately with the milk, mixing well after each addition. Stir in the flavorings. Spoon into a greased and floured tube pan. Bake at 325 degrees for 1 hour or until the cake tests done. Cool in the pan for 5 minutes. Invert onto a serving plate.

To prepare the glaze, combine the water and sugar in a saucepan. Bring to a boil and cook for 5 minutes or until the sugar dissolves, stirring constantly. Stir in the almond extract. Drizzle over the warm cake. This cake keeps fresh a long time because it is so rich. It can be baked in a bundt pan, but it will be more densely textured.

*Charlotte Ball*

# CREAM CHEESE POUND CAKE

1 cup (2 sticks) margarine, softened
1/2 cup (1 stick) butter, softened
8 ounces cream cheese, softened
3 cups sugar
6 eggs, lightly beaten
3 cups all-purpose flour
1 teaspoon vanilla extract

Cream the margarine, butter, cream cheese and sugar in a mixing bowl until light and fluffy. Beat in the eggs one at a time. Add the flour and beat until smooth. Stir in the vanilla. Spoon into a greased and floured tube pan. Place in a cold oven. Heat to 300 degrees and bake for 1 1/2 hours or until the cake tests done. Cool in the pan for 5 minutes. Invert onto a serving plate.

*Leigh Kitchens*

# GOOEY PUMPKIN BUTTER CAKE

1 (2-layer) package yellow cake mix
1/2 cup (1 stick) butter, melted
1 egg, lightly beaten
1 (15-ounce) can pumpkin
8 ounces cream cheese, softened
3 eggs, lightly beaten
1/2 cup (1 stick) butter, melted
1 teaspoon vanilla extract
1 (1-pound) package confectioners' sugar
2 teaspoons pumpkin pie spice

Combine the cake mix, 1/2 cup butter and 1 egg in a mixing bowl.
Beat at medium speed until smooth. Spread evenly in a lightly
greased 9×13-inch cake pan. Combine the pumpkin and cream cheese
in a mixing bowl and beat at low speed until smooth. Add 3 eggs,
1/2 cup butter and the vanilla and mix well. Add the confectioners'
sugar and pumpkin pie spice and mix well. Spread the pumpkin
mixture over the prepared layer. Bake at 350 degrees for 45 minutes.
The center of the cake should still be a little gooey.

*Becky James*

# RED VELVET CAKE

### CAKE
2 cups all-purpose flour
1 tablespoon baking cocoa
1/2 teaspoon salt
1/2 cup shortening
1 1/2 cups sugar
2 eggs, lightly beaten
1 cup buttermilk
2 ounces red food coloring
1 teaspoon vanilla extract
1 teaspoon baking soda
1 teaspoon vinegar

### BUTTER FROSTING
1 cup milk
1/3 cup all-purpose flour
Dash of salt
1/2 cup (1 stick) butter, softened
1/2 cup shortening
1 cup sugar
1 teaspoon vanilla

To prepare the cake, sift the flour, cocoa and salt together into a bowl. Cream the shortening and sugar in a mixing bowl until light and fluffy. Add the eggs and mix well. Add the flour mixture and buttermilk alternately, mixing well after each addition. Add the vanilla and food coloring and mix well. Stir in the baking soda and vinegar. Pour into two buttered 8-inch cake pans. Bake at 350 degrees for 30 minutes or until the cakes test done. Cool in the pans for 10 minutes. Remove to wire racks to cool completely.

To prepare the frosting, combine the milk, flour and salt in the top of a double boiler. Place the double boiler over boiling water and cook until the mixture is the consistency of pudding, stirring constantly. Remove from the heat and let stand until cool. Cream the butter, shortening and sugar in a mixing bowl until light and fluffy. Stir in the vanilla. Add the cooled milk mixture to the butter mixture and beat until smooth. Spread between the layers and over the top and side of the cake.

*Chris Sale*

# CHOCOLATE-COVERED CHERRIES

3 tablespoons butter or margarine, softened
3 tablespoons light corn syrup
1/4 teaspoon salt
2 cups sifted confectioners' sugar
60 maraschino cherries, drained
1 1/2 pounds dipping chocolate

Combine the butter, corn syrup and salt in a mixing bowl and beat until blended. Stir in the confectioners' sugar and knead until smooth. Chill if the sugar mixture is too soft. Shape 1 teaspoon of the sugar mixture around each cherry to enclose. Place on a baking sheet covered with waxed paper and chill. Place the chocolate in the top of a double boiler over simmering water. Cook until melted, stirring constantly. Dip the cherries one at a time into the chocolate, spooning chocolate over the cherries to coat completely. Return to the baking sheet and chill. Store in a covered container in the refrigerator for 1 to 2 weeks for enhanced flavor.

*Deana Trones*

# CHERRY MASH

2 cups sugar
2/3 cup evaporated milk
1/2 cup (1 stick) butter
12 large marshmallows
Dash of salt
1 small package cherry chips
1 teaspoon vanilla extract
2 cups (12 ounces) chocolate chips
3/4 cup peanut butter

Combine the sugar, evaporated milk, butter, marshmallows and salt in a saucepan and bring to a boil. Boil for 5 minutes, stirring constantly. Stir in the cherry chips and vanilla. Pour into a greased 9×13-inch baking pan. Combine the chocolate chips and peanut butter in the top of a double boiler over simmering water. Cook until the chocolate chips are melted, stirring constantly. Spread over the cherry mixture and let stand until cool. Cut into squares to serve.

*Chris Sale*

# FIVE-MINUTE FUDGE CIRCLE

1 (14-ounce) can sweetened condensed milk
2 cups (12 ounces) semisweet chocolate chips
1 cup butterscotch chips
1 teaspoon vanilla extract
8 ounces walnuts, chopped
Additional chopped walnuts

Pour the condensed milk into a saucepan, reserving the can. Add the chocolate chips, butterscotch chips and vanilla. Cook over low heat for about 3 minutes or until the chips are melted, stirring constantly. Stir in 8 ounces walnuts. Cover the reserved condensed milk can with plastic wrap and place in the center of a buttered 8-inch cake pan. Spoon the fudge into the pan to form a circle around the can. Push the can back to the center if necessary. (The fudge will be bumpy on top.) Sprinkle with additional walnuts and chill until firm. Remove the can and loosen the fudge from the side and bottom of the pan with a spatula. Cut into thin slices to serve. The fudge circle can be decorated with bows, ribbon or lace to make a Christmas wreath.

*Molly Castillo*

# Peanut Butter Balls

3 1/2 cups confectioners' sugar
1 1/3 cups creamy peanut butter
3/4 cup (1 1/2 sticks) margarine, softened
2 teaspoons vanilla extract
12 ounces chocolate chips
1 (4-ounce) bar paraffin

Combine the sugar, peanut butter, margarine and vanilla in a mixing bowl and beat at low speed until smooth. Shape the mixture into 1-inch balls. Place the chocolate chips and paraffin in the top of a double boiler over simmering water. Cook until melted, stirring constantly. Dip the peanut butter balls quickly in the chocolate mixture, coating entirely. Place on a baking sheet covered with waxed paper and chill until firm.

*Brian Shelton*

# LUSCIOUS BROWNIES

BROWNIES
1/2 cup (1 stick)
   margarine, melted
2 tablespoons baking cocoa
1 cup sugar
2 eggs, lightly beaten
3/4 cup all-purpose flour
Pinch of salt
1 cup pecans, chopped
1 (6-ounce) package miniature
   marshmallows

CHOCOLATE FROSTING
1/2 cup (1 stick) butter
6 tablespoons milk
3 tablespoons baking cocoa
1 (1-pound) package
   confectioners' sugar
1 teaspoon vanilla extract
1 cup pecans (optional)

To prepare the brownies, combine the margarine and baking cocoa in a small bowl and mix well. Blend the sugar and eggs in a mixing bowl. Add the cocoa mixture, flour and salt and beat until smooth. Stir in the pecans. Spoon into a 9×13-inch baking pan. Bake at 350 degrees for 20 minutes. Cover the top with the marshmallows. Bake until the marshmallows are puffy.

To prepare the frosting, combine the butter, milk and baking cocoa in a saucepan and mix well. Bring to a boil, stirring constantly. Remove from the heat and stir in the confectioners' sugar, vanilla and pecans. Pour over the hot brownies.

*Linda Hardin*

# Cinnamon Brownie Cake

BROWNIES
1 cup (2 sticks) margarine
1 cup water
1/4 cup baking cocoa
2 cups all-purpose flour
2 cups sugar
1/2 cup milk
2 eggs, lightly beaten
1 teaspoon vanilla extract
1 teaspoon cinnamon
1/2 teaspoon baking soda

CHOCOLATE FROSTING
1/2 cup milk
1/2 cup (1 stick) margarine
1/4 cup baking cocoa
1 (1-pound) package
    confectioners' sugar
1 teaspoon vanilla extract
1 cup chopped pecans

To prepare the brownies, combine the margarine, water and baking cocoa in a small saucepan and bring to a boil, stirring constantly. Pour into a mixing bowl. Add the flour and sugar and beat until smooth. Beat in the milk, eggs, vanilla, cinnamon and baking soda. Spoon into a 9×13-inch baking pan. Bake at 325 degrees for 25 minutes.

To prepare the frosting, combine the milk, margarine and baking cocoa in a saucepan and bring to a boil. Boil for 1 minute, stirring constantly. Remove from the heat and stir in the confectioners' sugar, vanilla and pecans. Pour over the warm brownies.

*Nan Yancey*

# BUTTERMILK BROWNIE CAKE

BROWNIES
2 cups all-purpose flour
2 cups sugar
1 teaspoon baking soda
1/2 teaspoon salt
1 cup (2 sticks) margarine
1 cup water
1/4 cup baking cocoa
1/2 cup buttermilk
2 eggs, lightly beaten
1 teaspoon vanilla extract

BUTTERMILK CHOCOLATE
FROSTING
1/2 cup (1 stick) margarine
6 tablespoons buttermilk
3 tablespoons baking cocoa
1 (1-pound) package
    confectioners'sugar
1 teaspoon vanilla extract
1 to 1 1/2 cups pecans
    (optional)

To prepare the brownies, sift the flour, sugar, baking soda and salt together into a mixing bowl. Combine the margarine, water and cocoa in a small saucepan and bring to a boil, stirring constantly. Pour immediately into the flour mixture and beat until blended. (The mixture will be thin.) Beat in the buttermilk, eggs and vanilla. Pour into a greased and floured 12×18-inch baking pan. Bake at 350 degrees for 25 minutes.

To prepare the frosting, combine the margarine, buttermilk and cocoa in a saucepan and bring to a boil. Remove from the heat and stir in the confectioners' sugar, vanilla and pecans. Pour over the warm brownies.

*Roger Harmon*

# CHOCOLATE MINT COOKIES

1 1/2 cups packed brown sugar
3/4 cup (1 1/2 sticks) butter or margarine
2 tablespoons water
2 cups (12 ounces) semisweet chocolate chips
2 eggs
2 1/2 cups all-purpose flour
1 1/4 teaspoons baking soda
1/2 teaspoon salt
Chocolate mint candies

Combine the brown sugar, butter and water in a medium saucepan.
Cook over medium-low heat until blended, stirring constantly.
Stir in the chocolate chips and cook until melted, stirring constantly.
Remove from the heat and let stand for 10 minutes. Combine the
flour, baking soda and salt in a large mixing bowl. Beat the eggs into
the chocolate mixture one at a time. Stir in the flour mixture.
Cover and chill for 1 hour.

Shape the chocolate mixture into 1-inch balls. Place about 2 inches
apart on a cookie sheet covered with ungreased foil. Bake at
350 degrees for 12 to 13 minutes. Remove from the oven and
immediately place one chocolate mint candy on top of each cookie.
Spread the melted candy over the top of each cookie with a knife.

These cookies will remind you of Girl Scout Thin Mints.

*Marla Storm*

# CHOCOLATE CHIP PUDDING COOKIES

2 1/4 cups all-purpose flour
1 teaspoon baking soda
1 cup (2 sticks) margarine, softened
3/4 cup packed brown sugar
1/4 cup granulated sugar
2 eggs, lightly beaten
1 (3-ounce) package vanilla or chocolate instant pudding mix
1 teaspoon vanilla extract
2 cups (12 ounces) chocolate chips

Mix the flour and baking soda in a bowl. Cream the margarine, brown sugar and granulated sugar in a mixing bowl until light and fluffy. Add the eggs and mix well. Add the flour mixture, pudding mix and vanilla and mix well. Stir in the chocolate chips. Drop by teaspoonfuls 2 inches apart onto a nonstick cookie sheet. Bake at 375 degrees for 8 to 10 minutes or until the edges are firm. Be careful not to overbake.

*Dawn Chaffee*

# No-Bake Chocolate Oatmeal Cookies

2 cups sugar
$1/2$ cup (1 stick) margarine, melted
$1/2$ cup milk
3 to 4 tablespoons baking cocoa
$2^1/2$ cups quick-cooking oats
$1/2$ cup chunky or smooth peanut butter
1 teaspoon vanilla

Combine the sugar, margarine, milk and cocoa in a saucepan and bring to a rolling boil. Boil and stir for $1^1/2$ minutes. Remove from the heat. Stir in the oats, peanut butter and vanilla. Drop by spoonfuls onto a cookie sheet covered with waxed paper. Let stand until firm, or chill to set more quickly.

*Roger Harmon*

# No-Bake Cookies

2 cups sugar
$^1$/2 cup milk
$^1$/2 cup (1 stick) butter
$^1$/4 cup baking cocoa
3 cups quick-cooking oats
$^1$/2 cup peanut butter
1 teaspoon vanilla extract
1 cup nuts (optional)
1 cup flaked coconut (optional)

Combine the sugar, milk, butter and cocoa in a saucepan and bring to a boil, stirring constantly. Remove from the heat. Stir in the oats, peanut butter, vanilla, nuts and coconut. Drop by spoonfuls onto a cookie sheet covered with waxed paper. Let stand until firm.

For a lighter cookie, use skim milk and reduced-fat peanut butter. Double the recipe to serve a large group.

*Ginger Holley*

# Cookies While You Sleep

2 egg whites, at room temperature
1/4 teaspoon cream of tartar
Pinch of salt
2/3 cup sugar
1 teaspoon vanilla extract
1/4 teaspoon almond extract
1 cup (6 ounces) chocolate chips
1 cup pecans (optional)

Beat the egg whites at low speed in a mixing bowl until foamy. Add the cream of tartar and salt and mix well. Beat in the sugar gradually. Add the flavorings and beat at medium-high speed until stiff peaks form. Fold in the chocolate chips and pecans. Drop by teaspoonfuls onto a cookie sheet covered with ungreased foil. Place in a preheated 350-degree oven and turn off the oven immediately. Let the cookies remain in the oven for 10 to 12 hours. Do not peek!

*Tracy Orwig*

# Oatmeal Butterscotch Cookies

1 cup (2 sticks) unsalted butter, softened
3/4 cup packed brown sugar
3/4 cup granulated sugar
2 eggs
1 teaspoon vanilla extract
1 teaspoon cinnamon
1 teaspoon baking soda
1/2 teaspoon salt
3 cups quick-cooking oats
1 1/2 cups all-purpose flour
1 2/3 cups butterscotch chips

Cream the butter, brown sugar and granulated sugar at medium speed in a mixing bowl until light and fluffy. Add the eggs and vanilla and mix well. Reduce the speed to low and beat in the cinnamon, baking soda and salt. Add the oats, flour and butterscotch chips gradually and mix well. Drop by teaspoonfuls onto an ungreased cookie sheet. Bake at 375 degrees for 8 minutes for chewy cookies or 9 to 10 minutes for crisp cookies. Cool on the cookie sheet for 3 minutes. Remove to a wire rack to cool completely.

*Jessica Murray*

# SEVEN-LAYER BARS

2 cups graham cracker crumbs
1/2 cup (1 stick) butter, melted
2 cups (12 ounces) chocolate chips
2 cups (12 ounces) butterscotch chips
3 cups chopped pecans or walnuts
3 cups shredded coconut
1 (14-ounce) can sweetened condensed milk

Mix the graham cracker crumbs and butter in a bowl. Spread in
a 9×13-inch baking pan. Layer the chocolate chips, butterscotch chips,
pecans and coconut over the crumb mixture in the order listed.
Drizzle the condensed milk over the top. Bake at 350 degrees for
30 minutes or until the coconut is as brown as desired. Cool.
Cut into squares.

*Jessica Murray*

# BLACK CHERRY MARZIPAN BARS

1 1/4 cups all-purpose flour
1/3 cup packed brown sugar
1/2 cup (1 stick)
  butter, softened
3/4 cup black cherry preserves
3/4 cup all-purpose flour
1/2 cup packed brown sugar

1/4 cup (1/2 stick)
  butter, softened
1 teaspoon almond extract
1/8 teaspoon salt
3/4 cup confectioners' sugar
1 tablespoon milk
1/2 teaspoon almond extract

Combine 1 1/4 cups flour, 1/3 cup brown sugar and 1/2 cup butter in a mixing bowl. Beat at low speed until crumbly. Pat into a greased and floured 9×9-inch baking pan. Bake at 350 degrees on the middle oven rack for 15 to 20 minutes or until the edges are light brown. Spread the preserves over the hot crust to within 1/4 inch of the edge.

Combine 3/4 cup flour, 1/2 cup brown sugar, 1/4 cup butter, 1 teaspoon almond extract and the salt in the mixing bowl. Beat at low speed until crumbly. Sprinkle over the preserves. Bake for 20 minutes or until the topping is light brown. Let stand until cool and then cut into two dozen small bars. Place on a serving plate.

Blend the confectioners' sugar, milk and 1/2 teaspoon almond extract in a small bowl. Drizzle over the bars.

*Janet Warren*

# Ooey Gooey Dessert Bars

1 (2-layer) package yellow cake mix
2 eggs, lightly beaten
1/2 cup (1 stick) butter, softened
1 (1-pound) package confectioners' sugar
8 ounces cream cheese, softened
2 eggs

Combine the cake mix, 2 eggs and the butter in a mixing bowl.
Pat into a greased 9×13-inch baking pan. Beat the confectioners'
sugar and the cream cheese in a mixing bowl until light and fluffy.
Add 2 eggs and mix well. Spread over the prepared layer. Bake at
350 degrees for 40 to 45 minutes or until set. Cool and cut
into bars.

*Deanna Barrow*

# SOPAIPILLA CHEESECAKE BARS

2 (8-count) cans refrigerator crescent rolls
16 ounces cream cheese, softened
1 cup sugar
1 teaspoon vanilla extract
1/2 cup cinnamon-sugar
1/2 cup (1 stick) butter, melted

Unroll one can of the crescent roll dough and place in a 9×13-inch baking dish coated with nonstick cooking spray, pressing to cover the bottom. Beat the cream cheese, sugar and vanilla in a mixing bowl until smooth. Spread over the dough. Unroll the remaining crescent roll dough onto a sheet of waxed paper and roll into a 9×13-inch rectangle. Place over the cream cheese mixture. Sprinkle with the cinnamon-sugar. Drizzle with the butter. Bake at 350 degrees for 25 to 30 minutes or until golden brown.

*Tracy Orwig*

# ALMOND CINNAMON CHEESECAKE BARS

2 (8-count) cans refrigerator crescent rolls
16 ounces cream cheese, softened
1 cup sugar
1/2 teaspoon vanilla extract
1/2 teaspoon almond extract
1/2 cup (1 stick) butter, melted
1/2 cup sugar
Cinnamon

Unroll one can of the crescent roll dough and place in a 9×13-inch baking dish coated with nonstick cooking spray, pressing to cover the bottom. Place the cream cheese in a large microwave-safe bowl. Microwave at 30-second intervals until the cream cheese can be stirred with a spoon. Add 1 cup sugar and the flavorings and stir until creamy. Spread over the dough. Unroll the remaining crescent roll dough on a sheet of waxed paper and roll into a 9×13-inch rectangle. Place over the cream cheese mixture. Drizzle with the butter. Sprinkle with 1/2 cup sugar. Sprinkle heavily with cinnamon. Bake at 350 degrees for 30 to 45 minutes or until golden brown. Cool and cut into bars.

This recipe can be prepared in advance and refrigerated before cutting into bars.

*Michael Law*

# Cookie Pizza

3/4 cup (1 1/2 sticks) butter or margarine, softened
1 cup sugar
1 egg
1 teaspoon vanilla extract
1 1/2 cups all-purpose flour
1/2 teaspoon baking soda
1/4 teaspoon salt
1/4 teaspoon baking cocoa
3/4 cup "M & M's" Chocolate Candies
1/2 cup miniature marshmallows

Cream the butter and sugar at medium speed in a mixing bowl until light and fluffy. Add the egg and vanilla and mix well. Add the flour, baking soda, salt and cocoa and mix well. Stir in 1/2 cup of the M & M's. Spoon onto a 12-inch pizza pan lined with greased heavy foil. Spread to within 1 inch of the edge. Bake at 350 degrees for 15 minutes. Sprinkle with the remaining 1/4 cup of the M & M's and the marshmallows. Bake for 5 to 7 more minutes or until the marshmallows are puffy and light brown. Cool on a wire rack. Cut into wedges to serve.

*Kathy Orwig*

# SPICE DROP COOKIES

1/2 cup (1 stick) margarine, softened
1 cup packed light brown sugar
1 egg, beaten
1 3/4 cups all-purpose flour
1 teaspoon baking soda
2 teaspoons cinnamon
1/2 teaspoon ground cloves
1/2 teaspoon salt
1 cup chopped walnuts or other nuts
1 cup raisins
1/2 cup buttermilk

Cream the margarine and brown sugar in a mixing bowl until light and fluffy. Add the egg and mix well. Sift the flour, baking soda, cinnamon, cloves and salt together into a bowl. Stir in the walnuts and raisins. Add the flour mixture and buttermilk to the sugar mixture alternately, mixing well after each addition. The batter will be stiff. Drop by teaspoonfuls 2 inches apart onto a greased cookie sheet. Bake at 375 degrees for 10 to 15 minutes or until firm around the edges.

*Kathy Filbert*

# Mom's Apple Pie

6 to 8 Granny Smith apples, peeled, cored and sliced
Juice of 1 lemon
2 cups all-purpose flour
3 tablespoons sugar
Dash of salt
2/3 cup vegetable oil
3 tablespoons milk

6 to 8 tablespoons butter
1/2 cup sugar
2 tablespoons all-purpose flour
1 teaspoon (heaping) cinnamon
3/4 cup all-purpose flour
1/2 cup sugar
1/3 cup butter

Place the apples and lemon juice in a bowl and cover with water. Combine 2 cups flour, 3 tablespoons sugar and the salt in a 9-inch pie plate and mix well. Whisk the oil and milk in a measuring cup until the oil is incorporated. Pour into the flour mixture and mix well. Press over the bottom and up the side of the pie plate. Trim and discard any excess dough. Drain the apples and spoon into the pastry. Dot with 6 to 8 tablespoons butter.

Combine 1/2 cup sugar, 2 tablespoons flour and the cinnamon and mix well. Sprinkle over the apples. Combine 3/4 cup flour and 1/2 cup sugar in a bowl. Cut in 1/3 cup butter with a pastry blender until the mixture resembles cornmeal. Sprinkle over the pie. Cover loosely with foil. Bake at 350 degrees for 45 minutes. Remove the foil and bake until golden brown.

*Margaret Dorland*

# Nana Ball's Famous Apple Pie

1 (2-crust) pie pastry
1 egg white, beaten
All-purpose flour
1/2 cup plus 1 tablespoon sugar
1 tablespoon arrowroot
1/4 teaspoon allspice
1 teaspoon cinnamon

6 to 8 Golden Delicious apples
  or any good cooking apple,
  peeled, cored and sliced
1 tablespoon butter
6 tablespoons evaporated milk
Sugar

Unfold one of the pastries into a pie plate. Fit the pastry into the plate and trim the edge. Brush the egg white over the bottom crust. Dust lightly with a small amount of flour and 1 tablespoon of the sugar. Combine the remaining 1 cup sugar, the arrowroot, allspice and cinnamon in a bowl. Toss the apples with the sugar mixture to coat. Spoon the apples into the pastry. Dot with the butter.

Roll the remaining pastry with a rolling pin on a lightly floured surface to make a slightly thinner than the bottom pastry. Place over the top of the pie, sealing the edge. Brush with the evaporated milk and sprinkle with additional sugar. Cut four to six vents in the pastry. Bake at 450 degrees on the lowest rack for 10 minutes. Turn the pie plate one-half turn and reduce the oven temperature to 375 degrees. Bake for 45 to 50 minutes or until golden brown. Cool on a wire rack. Serve with a large scoop of vanilla ice cream.

*Charlotte Ball*

# BUTTERMILK PIE

1/2 cup (1 stick) butter
2 cups sugar
3 eggs, beaten
1/4 cup all-purpose flour
1 cup buttermilk
1 teaspoon vanilla extract
Nutmeg to taste
1 unbaked (9-inch) pie shell

Cream the butter and sugar in a mixing bowl until light and fluffy.
Add the eggs and mix well. Add the flour, buttermilk, vanilla and
nutmeg and beat until smooth. Pour into the pie shell. Bake at
350 degrees for 45 to 50 minutes or until a knife inserted in the
center comes out clean.

*Becky James*

# PUMPKIN PIE

1/2 cup granulated sugar
1/2 cup packed brown sugar
1/4 cup all-purpose flour
1 teaspoon cinnamon
1/2 teaspoon ginger
1/2 teaspoon ground allspice
1/4 teaspoon salt
1 (15-ounce) can pumpkin
1/4 cup corn syrup
1 cup heavy cream
2 eggs, lightly beaten
1 unbaked (9-inch) deep-dish pie shell

Combine the granulated sugar, brown sugar, flour, cinnamon, ginger, allspice and salt in a mixing bowl and mix well. Blend the pumpkin and corn syrup in a bowl. Add to the sugar mixture and mix well. Add the cream and eggs and beat until smooth. Pour into the pie shell. Bake at 375 degrees for 45 minutes or until a knife inserted in the center comes out clean. Cool and serve with fresh whipped cream.

*Deana Trones*

# PECAN PUMPKIN PIE

PIE
1 (30-ounce) can pumpkin
  pie mix
1 cup sugar
1 (5-ounce) can evaporated
  milk
3 eggs, lightly beaten
2 teaspoons cinnamon
1/2 teaspoon salt

1 (2-layer) package yellow
  cake mix
1 cup (2 sticks) butter, melted
1 1/2 cups chopped pecans

CARAMEL SAUCE
1 cup (2 sticks) butter
2 cups packed brown sugar
1 cup whipping cream

To prepare the pie, line two 9-inch pie plates with waxed paper or baking parchment and coat the paper with nonstick cooking spray. Combine the pumpkin pie mix, sugar and evaporated milk in a mixing bowl and beat until smooth. Beat in the eggs, cinnamon and salt. Pour evenly into the prepared pie plates. Sprinkle with the cake mix and drizzle with the butter. Sprinkle with the pecans and press down lightly. Bake at 350 degrees for 50 to 60 minutes or until golden brown. Cool on a wire rack for 2 hours. Loosen the pie from the side of the pan. Invert onto a serving plate. Remove the waxed paper and chill.

To prepare the sauce, melt the butter in a heavy saucepan over low heat. Add the brown sugar and cream. Cook until the brown sugar is dissolved, stirring constantly. Drizzle the warm sauce over each slice of pie and add a dollop of whipped topping.

*Margaret Dorland*

# CHOCOLATE PECAN PIE

2/3 cup evaporated milk
2 tablespoons all-purpose flour
2 tablespoons butter or margarine
1 cup (6 ounces) chocolate chips, or
    6 tablespoons baking cocoa
1 cup sugar
1/2 cup corn syrup
2 eggs, lightly beaten
1 teaspoon vanilla extract
1/4 teaspoon salt
1 cup whole or chopped pecans
1 unbaked (9-inch) pie shell

Combine the evaporated milk, flour, butter and chocolate chips in a small saucepan. Cook over low heat until the butter and chocolate chips are melted, stirring constantly. Remove from the heat. Combine the sugar, corn syrup, eggs, vanilla, salt and pecans in a mixing bowl. Stir in the chocolate mixture. Pour into the pie shell. Bake at 375 degrees for 35 to 40 minutes or until the crust is golden brown. Serve warm or cold.

*Patrick Hughes*

# Sweet Endings Chocolate Bourbon Pecan Pie

3/4 cup packed light brown sugar
3/4 cup light corn syrup
6 tablespoons butter, melted and cooled
3 eggs
1 tablespoon bourbon
1 1/2 teaspoons vanilla extract
3/4 cup chocolate chips
1 unbaked (9-inch) deep-dish pie shell
3/4 cup pecan halves

Combine the brown sugar, corn syrup and butter in a mixing bowl and mix well. Add the eggs one at a time, mixing well after each addition. Beat until light and fluffy. Stir in the bourbon and vanilla. Sprinkle the chocolate chips in the pie shell. Sprinkle the pecans over the chocolate chips. Pour the filling over the pecans. Bake at 350 degrees for 45 to 50 minutes or until the filling is set.

*Deana Trones*

# MALT SHOP PIE

1 pint vanilla ice cream, softened
1/2 cup chocolate malt balls, crushed
1 tablespoon chocolate malt powder
1 (9-inch) graham cracker pie shell
1 cup whipped topping
3 tablespoons chocolate malt powder
1 tablespoon marshmallow creme
Crushed chocolate malt balls

Combine the ice cream, 1/2 cup malt balls and 1 tablespoon malt powder in a bowl and mix well. Spoon into the pie shell. Freeze until firm. Keep frozen until ready to serve.

Mix the whipped topping, 3 tablespoons malt powder and the marshmallow crème in a small bowl. Spoon over the frozen pie. Sprinkle with additional crushed malt balls and serve.

*Tracy Orwig*

# Hershey Pie

16 ounces chocolate, melted
16 ounces whipped topping
$^1/_2$ cup pecans, chopped
1 unbaked (9-inch) pie shell
8 ounces whipped topping

Combine the chocolate and 16 ounces whipped topping and mix well. Stir in the pecans. Spoon into the pie shell. Chill. Top with 8 ounces whipped topping before serving.

*Linda Hardin*

# Sinful Pie Dessert

1 1/2 cups all-purpose flour
3/4 cup (1 1/2 sticks) butter, melted
1 cup pecans, chopped
8 ounces cream cheese
1 1/2 cups confectioners' sugar
8 ounces whipped topping
2 (6-ounce) packages chocolate instant pudding mix
3 1/2 cups milk
Chopped pecans

Mix the flour and butter in a bowl. Stir in the pecans. Press into a 9×13-inch baking dish. Bake at 375 degrees for 20 minutes. Cool.

Blend the cream cheese, confectioners' sugar and one-half of the whipped topping in a mixing bowl. Spread over the crust. Mix the pudding mix and milk in a bowl. Pour over the cream cheese mixture. Spread the remaining whipped topping over the pudding. Sprinkle generously with additional pecans. Chill in the refrigerator.

*Ruth Ann Lisotta*

# APPRECIATION APPLE DUMPLINGS

1 (8-count) can refrigerator crescent rolls
1 Granny Smith apple, peeled, cored and cut into 8 wedges
1/2 cup (1 stick) butter, melted
2/3 cup sugar
Cinnamon
1 (8-ounce) can Mountain Dew

Unroll the crescent roll dough and separate into triangles. Place one apple wedge near the wide edge of each triangle of dough. Roll to enclose the apple, pressing to seal. Arrange in a 9×13-inch baking pan coated with nonstick cooking spray. Mix the butter and sugar in a small bowl and spoon over the dumplings. Sprinkle with cinnamon. Pour the Mountain Dew in a corner of the pan. Bake at 350 degrees for 30 minutes or until golden brown.

*Liz Roberts*

# GRILLED BANANAS

4 large bananas
$1/4$ cup ($1/2$ stick) butter, melted
$1/2$ cup packed brown sugar
2 tablespoons cinnamon
1 teaspoon nutmeg

Cut the bananas into halves lengthwise, leaving the peel on. Brush the cut sides with the butter. Mix the brown sugar, cinnamon and nutmeg in a small bowl. Sprinkle over the cut sides of the bananas and press gently. Place the bananas cut side down on a grill rack. Grill over high heat for 2 to 4 minutes to caramelize the sugar. Turn over the bananas. Grill skin side down until the skin separates from the banana. Remove from the heat and serve immediately with ice cream.

*Chris Sale*

# BANANA PUDDING

1 (6-ounce) package vanilla instant pudding mix
1 (14-ounce) can sweetened condensed milk
8 ounces cream cheese, softened
8 ounces whipped topping
Vanilla wafers
6 bananas, sliced

Prepare the pudding mix in a large mixing bowl using the package directions. Add the condensed milk and cream cheese and beat until smooth. Fold in one-half of the whipped topping. Alternate layers of vanilla wafers, pudding mixture and bananas in a serving dish. Top with the remaining whipped topping.

*Lou Ann Condon*

# BREAD PUDDING

PUDDING
15 slices bread, torn into
  pieces
1³/4 cups milk
6 eggs, lightly beaten
3 cups sugar
1 tablespoon vanilla extract
Pinch of salt
¹/2 cup (1 stick) butter
Cinnamon to taste

RUM SAUCE
2 cups sugar
¹/2 cup (1 stick) butter
1 tablespoon vanilla extract
Rum to taste
1¹/2 cups whipping cream

To prepare the pudding, arrange the bread in a 9×13-inch baking pan coated with nonstick cooking spray. Pour the milk over the bread. Combine the eggs, sugar, vanilla and salt in a mixing bowl and beat until smooth. Pour over the bread and stir gently. Dot evenly with the butter. Sprinkle with cinnamon. Bake at 350 degrees for 30 minutes; stir. Bake for 30 to 40 more minutes or until golden brown.

To prepare the sauce, combine the sugar, butter, vanilla and rum in a saucepan. Bring to a boil, stirring constantly. Remove from the heat and let stand for about 10 minutes. Stir in the whipping cream. Return to the stove and heat just until boiling; do not allow to boil over. Pour over the bread pudding.

This sauce is also great over ice cream. You may use brandy, whiskey or imitation flavoring instead of the rum.

*Melinda Wright*

# PETITE CHERRY CHEESECAKES

16 ounces cream cheese, softened
3/4 cup sugar
2 eggs, lightly beaten
1 tablespoon lemon juice
1 teaspoon vanilla extract
24 vanilla wafers
1 (21-ounce) can cherry pie filling

Beat the cream cheese, sugar, eggs, lemon juice and vanilla in a mixing bowl until light and fluffy. Line twenty-four muffin cups with paper baking cups and place a vanilla wafer in each. Fill the muffin cups two-thirds full with the cream cheese mixture. Bake at 375 degrees for 15 to 20 minutes. Top evenly with the pie filling.

*Chris Sale*

# CINNAMON LOGS

1 (1-pound) loaf thinly sliced white bread
8 ounces cream cheese, softened
1/2 cup confectioners' sugar
1 egg white
1 cup granulated sugar
1 tablespoon cinnamon
1 cup (2 sticks) butter, melted

Trim the crusts from the bread slices. Roll 1/4 inch thick on a work surface. Beat the cream cheese, confectioners' sugar and egg white at medium speed in a mixing bowl until smooth. Spread evenly on one side of each bread slice. Roll each slice into a log. Mix the granulated sugar and cinnamon in a shallow bowl. Dip the logs one at a time in the melted butter in a bowl. Roll in the cinnamon-sugar to coat. Arrange on a lightly greased baking sheet. Bake at 350 degrees for 15 minutes.

*Margaret Dorland*

# CRANBERRY RUGALACH

1 cup (2 sticks) unsalted
  butter, softened
8 ounces Neufchâtel
  cheese, softened
1/2 cup sugar
2 3/4 cups all-purpose flour
1 teaspoon salt
1 1/4 cups sugar

7 tablespoons unsalted
  butter, melted
2 3/4 teaspoons cinnamon
1 1/2 teaspoons allspice
1 1/4 cups dried cranberries,
  chopped
1 1/4 cups walnuts, chopped
1 egg, beaten

Combine the butter, cheese and 1/2 cup sugar in a large mixing bowl and beat until light and fluffy. Add the flour and salt and mix well. Shape the dough into a ball and knead for 30 seconds. Divide into eight equal portions. Flatten each portion into an 8-inch circle. Wrap each circle of dough with plastic wrap and chill for 1 hour. (The dough can also be made in advance and refrigerated for up to 24 hours.)

Blend 1 1/4 cups sugar, 7 tablespoons butter, the cinnamon and allspice in a small bowl. Stir in the cranberries and walnuts. Place the dough one circle at a time on a work surface, keeping the remainder in the refrigerator. Spread 1/4 cup of the filling over each circle, leaving a 1/2-inch border. Cut each circle into eight wedges. Roll the dough tightly from the wide ends to enclose the filling. Shape into crescents and place point side down on an ungreased cookie sheet. Brush the cookies with the egg. Sprinkle with additional sugar. Bake on the center rack of the oven at 350 degrees for 20 minutes or until light brown. Cool. Store in an airtight container at room temperature; do not store with other cookies.

These cookies can be frozen in an airtight container for up to 1 month.

*Janet Warren*

# MOCK ÉCLAIRS

2 (3-ounce) packages vanilla instant pudding mix
3 cups milk
8 ounces whipped topping
1 (16-ounce) box graham crackers
2 ounces unsweetened chocolate
3 tablespoons butter
1 1/2 cups confectioners' sugar
3 tablespoons milk
2 tablespoons light corn syrup
1 teaspoon vanilla extract

Combine the pudding mix and 3 cups milk in a bowl and mix well.
Let stand until set. Stir in the whipped topping. Alternate layers
of the graham crackers and pudding mixture in a 9×13-inch baking
pan, beginning and ending with the graham crackers.

Melt the chocolate in a saucepan over low heat. Remove from the
heat. Add the butter and stir until melted. Pour into a mixing bowl.
Add the confectioners' sugar, 3 tablespoons milk, the corn syrup
and vanilla and beat until smooth. Spread over the graham crackers.
Chill for 12 to 24 hours.

*Terry Suchala*

# Flan

1 3/4 cups whipping cream
1 cup whole milk
Pinch of salt
1/2 vanilla bean, cut into
   halves lengthwise

1 cup sugar
1/3 cup water
3 eggs, lightly beaten
2 egg yolks, lightly beaten
7 tablespoons sugar

Combine the cream, milk and salt in a heavy saucepan and mix well. Scrape the seeds from the vanilla bean into the saucepan. Stir in the bean. Bring to a simmer over medium heat. Remove from the heat and let stand for 30 minutes.

Cook 1 cup sugar and the water in a heavy saucepan over low heat until the sugar dissolves, stirring constantly. Increase the heat to high. Cook without stirring for about 10 minutes or until the syrup turns deep amber in color, brushing down the side of the pan with a wet pastry brush and swirling the pan occasionally. Pour the caramel syrup quickly into six 3/4-cup ramekins or custard cups. Tilt and turn each ramekin to coat the sides. Place in a 9×13-inch baking pan.

Whisk the eggs, egg yolks and 7 tablespoons sugar in a bowl until blended. Whisk the cream mixture gradually and gently into the egg mixture, being careful not to create much foam. Pour through a small sieve into the ramekins until full, discarding the solids. Pour enough hot water into the baking dish to come halfway up the sides of the ramekins. Bake on the center oven rack at 350 degrees for 40 minutes or until the centers of the flans are set but not firm. Remove the ramekins from the baking dish and place on a wire rack to cool. Chill for about 2 hours. Cover and chill for 10 to 12 hours longer. The flans can be made in advance and refrigerated for up to 48 hours before serving.

Loosen the flans from the sides of the ramekins with a small sharp knife. Invert onto a serving plate, shaking gently to release. Lift off the ramekin gently and allow the caramel syrup to run over the flan.

*Jessica Murray*

# Lemon Panna Cotta with Blueberry Sauce

## Panna Cotta
1 envelope unflavored gelatin
1 cup milk
1/2 cup plus 2 tablespoons sugar
3 cups low-fat buttermilk
1 teaspoon grated lemon zest

## Blueberry Sauce
1/2 cup apple juice
1/4 cup sugar
1 tablespoon fresh lemon juice
2 cups fresh blueberries

To prepare the panna cotta, sprinkle the gelatin over the milk in a small saucepan and let stand for 10 minutes. Cook over medium-low heat for 10 minutes, whisking constantly. Increase the heat to medium and then add the sugar. Cook until the sugar dissolves, stirring constantly. Stir in the buttermilk and lemon zest. Pour into custard cups coated with nonstick cooking spray. Chill for at least 5 hours. Invert onto dessert plates.

To prepare the sauce, combine the apple juice, sugar and lemon juice in a small saucepan. Bring to a boil. Cook until the sugar dissolves, stirring constantly. Reduce the heat to medium and stir in the blueberries. Cook for 8 minutes or until the blueberries are warm and begin to pop. Remove from the heat. Cool to room temperature. Serve with the panna cotta.

*Jessica Murray*

# Fresh Peach Cobbler

1/3 cup packed brown sugar
1 tablespoon cinnamon
2 teaspoons cornstarch
1/4 teaspoon vanilla extract
6 to 8 large peaches, peeled and sliced
1 cup granulated sugar
2/3 cup all-purpose flour
1 teaspoon cinnamon
1/2 cup (1 stick) unsalted butter, cut into small pieces
1/2 cup chopped pecans

Combine the brown sugar, 1 tablespoon cinnamon, the cornstarch
and vanilla in a bowl and mix well. Add the peaches and toss
to coat. Spoon into an ungreased baking pan. Mix the granulated
sugar, flour and 1 teaspoon cinnamon in a bowl. Cut in the butter
until crumbly. Stir in the pecans. Sprinkle over the peaches. Bake at
350 degrees for 45 minutes or until golden brown and bubbly.

To prepare ahead, you may chill the topping and peaches separately.
Bring to room temperature before assembling and baking.

*Jessica Murray*

# STRAWBERRY SQUARES

1 cup all-purpose flour
1/4 cup packed brown sugar
1/2 cup (1 stick) butter, melted
1/2 cup chopped walnuts
1 (10-ounce) package frozen strawberries, thawed
2/3 cup granulated sugar
2 egg whites
2 tablespoons lemon juice
8 ounces whipped topping

Combine the flour and brown sugar in a bowl. Add the butter and mix well. Stir in the walnuts. Spoon into a shallow baking pan. Bake at 350 degrees for 20 minutes, stirring frequently. Combine the strawberries, granulated sugar, egg whites and lemon juice in a mixing bowl. Beat at high speed for 10 minutes. Fold in the whipped topping. Spoon two-thirds of the flour mixture into a 9×13-inch baking pan. Spoon the strawberry mixture over the prepared layer. Top with the remaining flour mixture. Freeze for at least 6 hours before serving.

*Pam Hite*

# THE BROWN BENTLEY

1 pint vanilla ice cream, slightly softened
3 to 4 tablespoons Kahlúa, or to taste
3 to 4 tablespoons crème de cacao, or to taste

Combine the ice cream, Kahlúa and crème de cacao in a blender and process until smooth. Pour into dessert glasses and garnish with sliced strawberries and a wafer cookie.

*Charlotte Ball*

# INDEX

Molly Castillo

Telephone (972) 542-5302

Fax (972) 569-9988

www.TheSamaritanInn.org

All proceeds from this cookbook will support The Samaritan Inn,
a comprehensive, not-for-profit program for the homeless that provides
refuge, counseling, vocational training, and life-skill classes—all designed
to support people in their quest to regain their independence.